NAVIGATE LIFE LIKE A PRO

100 DAYS FOR BOYS TO BUILD CONFIDENCE AND PURPOSE

ZONDERKIDZ

Navigate Life Like a Pro: 100 Days for Boys to Build Confidence and Purpose

Portions of this book adapted from *The Ultimate Devo for Boys* (ISBN: 97803104534) Copyright © 2007, 2000 by Ed Strauss

Published in Grand Rapids, Michigan, by Zonderkidz. Zonderkidz is a registered trademark of The Zondervan Corporation, L.L.C., a wholly owned subsidiary of HarperCollins Christian Publishing, Inc.

Requests for information should be addressed to customercare@harpercollins.com.

ISBN 9780310177739 (softcover)
ISBN 9780310177746 (ebook)
ISBN 9780310177753 (audio)

Library of Congress Control Number: 2025948011

Zondervan titles may be purchased in bulk for educational, business, fundraising, or sales promotional use. For information, please email SpecialMarkets@Zondervan.com.

Cover Illustration: Juicebox Designs
Interior Design: Mallory Collins
Written by Ed Strauss

Printed in the United States of America

26 27 28 29 30 LBC 5 4 3 2 1

DAY 1

YOUNG AND FUN LOVING

Don't let anyone look down on you because you are young, but set an example for the believers in speech, in conduct, in love, in faith and in purity.

1 TIMOTHY 4:12

Timothy was a young man when he joined Paul's team. Timothy was timid, but God saw that he had the right stuff and later made him a leader of the churches. Only problem was, Timothy was still so young. Many older Christians thought young meant immature, so Paul told Timothy to prove that this wasn't true by setting an example of living as a Christian.

What does this mean for you? Does it mean that being a Christian is super-serious business and that you should never laugh, never have goofy moments and never enjoy any wild, energetic fun? Does it mean you have to try to be perfect? No, it doesn't mean any of that. But being young and fun loving does not equal being foolish and out-of-control.

Live for the truth and give careful thought to how you speak and behave. You may be full of energy and jokes, but don't let go completely so that you become outrageously foolish and disrespectful like a baboon that's throwing stuff at the crowds watching him. Yes, have fun, but remember how God expects all Christians—young and old—to behave.

More people are watching your life than you imagine. Don't give them any reason to look down on you or the faith you believe in.

Write down some examples of how you can be a positive example for your faith.

DAY 2

SEEING THAT GOD IS REAL

God's invisible qualities—his eternal power and divine nature—have been clearly seen, being understood from what has been made.

ROMANS 1:20

God is a spiritual being. He lives in another dimension, and human eyes just aren't made for seeing spiritual things. That whole realm is invisible to us. But there is a way to clearly understand what he's like. How's that? By looking at the world that God made.

When you play a super-cool computer game with cutting-edge graphics, you just know that some awesome programmer designed the thing, right? Even if the programmer's not around for you to actually see, you know he or she exists. If you walk into your friend's house and see a million-piece Lego castle, you might ask, "Whoa! Did you build this?" If your friend says,

"Nah. The dog sneezed, and this all fell into place," you'd say, "Yeah, riiight."

It's the same with God. Study the awesome way that nature works and how complex living things are, and it hits you that you're looking at the work of an invisible, intelligent Creator.

And this Creator's not just super smart; he also has awesome power. When people examine things like DNA or the human brain, even if they don't know God, they figure there had to be an intelligent designer behind it. It's far too amazing to be an accident.

Do you want to see evidence of God? Look at the things he created. They tell you a lot about what he's like and give you a glimpse of how powerful he is.

When you look at creation where do you see evidence of God most clearly?

DAY 3

JESUS' POWERFUL RESURRECTION

He was not abandoned to the realm of the dead, nor did his body see decay. God has raised this Jesus to life, and we are all witnesses of it.

ACTS 2:31-32

Jesus was nailed to a cross on a Friday morning, and he died that afternoon. His friends buried him just before sunset, and Jesus' lifeless body lay in a cold, dark tomb all that night, all the next day, and all the next night. Then at dawn Sunday morning, there was a violent earthquake, the stone door of his tomb rolled aside, and Jesus walked out. He appeared to his disciples, proving that he was alive again.

You may say, "Okay, I saw a program on TV about a guy whose heart stopped. He was dead for two minutes, and then the doctors gave him an electric shock, and he came back to life." Yeah, but that guy wasn't nearly beaten to death by

Roman soldiers and then nailed to a cross. And he didn't lie dead in a tomb for about forty hours. When people are dead like Jesus was dead, they stay dead.

Another thing: When Jesus' body came back to life, his flesh-and-blood corpse was transformed into a powerful, eternal body that could walk through walls or appear and disappear. His body had been utterly changed. This was a supernatural miracle.

Jesus is the only person who ever actually died, rose from the dead, and now lives forever! His resurrection was huge, convincing proof that he was who he claimed to be—God's Son.

In your own words, how would you describe Jesus to a curious friend?

DAY 4

LOOKS AREN'T EVERYTHING

In all Israel there was not a man so highly praised for his handsome appearance as Absalom.

2 SAMUEL 14:25

King David was a very handsome guy, and he married Maacah, the drop-dead gorgeous princess of Geshur. Well, no big surprise that their son Absalom was so good-looking! From the top of his head to the end of his big toe, there wasn't a blemish on him. There wasn't even one freckle out of place. Problem was, Absalom was in love with how he looked. He thought his hair was so cool, he let it grow down past his waist. He had five pounds of curly locks!

Absalom's outside might have been picture-perfect, but his heart was seriously messed up. This is the guy who killed his older brother, tried to murder his father, and took advantage of ten women up on the palace roof where everyone could see them. Whoa! Talk about a mess! If you think that Absalom sounds like a Hollywood star with his life out of control, you got that one right! Some dudes don't make good role models no matter what kind of celebrity they are.

It's nice if you're good-looking, but that really isn't the important thing. If you don't know right from wrong, looks don't count for much. Are you ready for this one? The Bible says that a good-looking person with no morals is like a gold ring stuck through the snotty snout of a pig (Proverbs 11:22)!

You can be plain, or you can be a looker; it really doesn't matter. What's important is to have godly character.

Why is godly character more beneficial than good looks?

DAY 5

THE HOLY SPIRIT'S POWER

You will receive power when the Holy Spirit comes on you.

ACTS 1:8

What's this? Receiving power? That sounds good—like a superpower! But who is this Holy Spirit? The Holy Spirit is also called the Spirit of God, and Jesus promised his disciples that after he went to heaven he'd send the Spirit of God himself into their hearts—to live inside them! Wow! No wonder you get power! When God's Spirit enters you, you admit the most powerful being in the universe into your life.

There are lots of movies and cartoons about kids receiving superpowers. Someone gets bombarded with radiation, or a genetically altered spider bites him, and the next thing you know he can walk up walls, bend steel bars, or surround himself with a force field. Of course, on top of going to school and doing homework, these superheroes have to wear colorful costumes and go out and save the world!

Although superheroes aren't real, what the Bible says about God filling you with the power of his Holy Spirit is real. Of course, God probably won't give you the ability to climb up skyscrapers. God gives his Spirit so that you'll have power to live like a Christian. His Spirit also comforts you when you're afraid or sad. The Holy Spirit teaches you how to pray and guides you in your choices. The Spirit also helps you tell others about Jesus.

God's Spirit can give you power, and you need that power. So, pray and ask God to help you access the power of the Holy Spirit, so you can begin to live a stronger Christian life.

What are some ways you can remind yourself that the Holy Spirit is present and able to help you live a Christian life?

DAY 6

RIPPED ISN'T ENOUGH

Let not . . . the strong boast of their strength . . . but let the one who boasts boast about this: that they have understanding to know me, that I am the Lord.

JEREMIAH 9:23-24

God had just finished telling the Israelites that disaster was going to hit their land and there was nothing they could do to stop it. The enemy was going to invade their land and smash into their fortresses. The Israelites could boast till they were blue in the face about how strong they were, but they weren't anywhere near strong enough to stop what was coming. Only God could protect them.

If you're tough, don't lie and say, "Oh man, look at me! I'm a pitiful weakling." If you're strong and you know that you're strong, have a healthy self-confidence. Know that kids can't push you around. If tough situations come up, be confident that you can face them. There's nothing wrong with that. God wants you to be strong.

But don't go around boasting about how strong you are, because no matter how tough you are, you can't handle all the heavy stuff life sends your way. A lot of things are so big that you can't protect yourself from them. If you depend on your muscles alone, you'll go under. But realize that you have your limits and that you need God to protect you, and you'll make it.

God is strongest of all. When you can't handle stuff, trust him to take care of it.

Describe a time when you had to rely on God's strength rather than your own. How did things turn out?

DAY 7

A WISE MAN'S ATTITUDE

Do not rebuke mockers or they will hate you; rebuke the wise and they will love you.

PROVERBS 9:8

Why, when you think of a certain kid, would you describe him as a mocker? Well, these days you probably wouldn't. Instead, you'd say, "Man, does that kid have a mouth on him!" Or, "What a know-it-all!" Back in Bible days they had a simple name for a kid like that—mocker. No matter what you tried to tell this kid, he'd mock you.

Try to set him straight on something, and he just hates you. Why should he listen? He knows it all already. Of course, he doesn't, but he's so defensive and proud that he can't bear to listen to any kind of correction. So he tries to act smart and uses sarcastic humor to attack anyone who tries to straighten him out. You learn quickly not to try to tell him anything.

A know-it-all is a pain to be around. So be wise. When your friends try to teach you how not to goof up, or your parents rebuke you after you've blown it, listen to what they say and learn from it. It'll keep you from making the same mistake again. When someone goes to the trouble to correct you, it shows they care about you.

Don't get into it with a mocker, and don't be a mocker yourself. You'll learn a lot more and be a lot easier to live with if you're willing to listen to correction.

Describe the traits of a mocker or a know-it-all. Why is it wise to avoid that behavior?

DAY 8

DON'T LET THE BULL LOOSE!

Do not do anything that endangers your neighbor's life.

LEVITICUS 19:16

Now, there's a commonsense law that makes sense, huh? It's simple and to the point. But God didn't stop there. Most people really need things spelled out, so God spelled them out: If you have a mean bull that has a bad habit of goring people with its horns, keep *el toro* locked up in a pen (Exodus 21:29). Do not let the bull loose, whatever you do!

Some kids can't stand rules. They just wanna cut loose and go out and have fun. Yeah, but if you don't obey common-sense rules, you endanger other people's lives. You might leap off the diving board right on top of another swimmer. Ignore the maximum-number-of-kids-on-a-trampoline rule, and you'll bounce some kid off the trampoline onto his head. Every summer, lots of kids are rushed from pools and trampolines to the hospital. Rules are there for a reason.

You may wonder why God put so many laws in the Bible—especially in the Old Testament. He did it because he loves people and doesn't want to see them hurt. That's why he wrote laws to protect people's property—so someone couldn't just come along and take what didn't belong to them. That's why he wrote laws against stealing and lying and cheating others. That's why he made laws about being kind to other people.

You're smart to obey God's laws. It's great if you understand why the rules exist. But even if you don't understand, remember, God put rules there to protect you and others.

Write down some rules that protect you and others. What do you think it would be like if there were no rules or laws?

DAY 9

CHECKING YOUR MOTIVES

The LORD searches every heart and understands every desire and every thought.

1 CHRONICLES 28:9

God hears every word you speak. He knows every thought you think. And get this: He knows the motives behind every thought you think. God shines a light into your heart, checking out what motivates you, what makes you do what you do. You can't hide anything from him! No wonder King David said, "Before a word is on my tongue you, LORD, know it completely" (Psalm 139:4). You bet God does! He knew what you were going to say before you even thought it.

At the end of your life when you stand before the judgment seat of Christ, you'll be rewarded for all the good you've done, and all the garbage will be burned away. At that time, you'll be asked to give an account to God for every thoughtless word you've said. Jesus said that if you even think of sinning, it's as if you've already done the deed.

What effect does it have on you to know that God knows the motives behind your actions? Don't let it worry you. Sure, you should have a healthy respect for God, but more than anything, double-check your motives. Ask God to forgive you when you slip up. He loves you, and he's on your side!

God knows absolutely everything you do, say, think, or think about thinking. That's a good reason to do good, speak good, and even think good.

What evidence do you see that leads you to believe that God is on your side and pulling for you?

DAY 10

TALKING TO GOD ALL DAY LONG

Pray continually, give thanks in all circumstances; for this is God's will for you in Christ Jesus.

1 THESSALONIANS 5:17–18

Pray continually? Does that mean I'm supposed to stumble around on my knees with my eyes shut? Nice try, buddy. You won't even make it across the street if you try that stunt. Praying continually means that you can talk to God no matter what you're doing. And prayer isn't just asking God for stuff. Often it's a quick thank-you to God. Sometimes it simply means being aware of God and wanting to obey him.

When you hear the words "prayer time," what comes to your mind? Saying twenty seconds' worth of grace over leftover pasta? Yawning bedside prayers for forty seconds? Those things are prayer, true, but with 1,440 minutes in a day, don't you have more time for God than one minute? God is your best friend, and he's with you all day long. If you spent all day with one of your friends, you'd talk to him a lot, right?

So communicate with God. He wants to hear from you. Prayer is talking honestly and respectfully to God, and you should do that no matter what else you're doing—whether you're lying down to sleep, making a tough decision, or white-water rafting with your eyes wide open. Yes, it's okay to pray with your eyes open.

God is always here listening, and he has the power to answer your prayers. So stay in close communication with him.

▶ **How would you describe your prayer life? How can you remind yourself to pause and pray throughout the day?**

GOD IS ALWAYS HERE LISTENING, AND HE HAS THE POWER TO ANSWER YOUR PRAYERS. SO STAY IN CLOSE COMMUNICATION WITH HIM.

DAY 11

ONE GOD—ONE WAY TO HEAVEN

Salvation is found in no one else, for there is no other name under heaven given to mankind by which we must be saved.

ACTS 4:12

If you want to please God and live forever in heaven, first you have to figure out who God is. So, who is the true god? Were the ancient Greeks right when they said that when you leave this life you will live in Elysium with Zeus? Nope. Well then, how about the ancient Scandinavians who said that you will live in Valhalla with Thor? No. This verse tells us that there's only one God who brings salvation—the God of the Bible. All other so-called gods are imposters.

Now, how do you find salvation with the one true God? What do you have to do to make sure that you end up in heaven? If you brush your teeth faithfully four hundred times a day, rake leaves off every driveway in your city, and rescue at least forty cats from trees, will that do it? No. Those things will wear you out, but they won't get you into heaven. So what's the way?

Jesus said, "I am the way." He added, "No one comes to the Father except through me" (John 14:6). Okay, now we're zeroing in on how to find salvation. You have to go through Jesus! In fact, the Bible makes it very clear: "If you declare with your mouth, 'Jesus is Lord,' and believe in your heart that God raised him from the dead, you will be saved" (Romans 10:9).

Praying to Zeus won't save you. Being the best Boy Scout on the block won't save you. Only believing in Jesus gives you eternal life.

Have you trusted Jesus as your Savior? If not, what is holding you back?

DAY 12

CONTROLLING THE HEAT VENTS

Fools give full vent to their rage, but the wise bring calm in the end.

PROVERBS 29:11

Have you ever heard the phrase "give full vent"? What does it mean to give "full vent" to our anger? Giving full vent means to really let'er rip—tell 'em what's on your mind with as much direct honesty as you can manage. Not advised. A wise man deals with problems, yes, but he keeps his anger under control so no one gets burned.

Maybe you have a short fuse and you're easily angered. Or maybe it's only certain kids who get under your skin and annoy you.

Even when we've been provoked, the Bible says, "Everyone should be . . . slow to become angry" (James 1:19). Don't give full vent to your anger. Here's an interesting test to help you see what a big deal self-control is in the Bible. If you or someone you know has a thing in their Bible called a concordance (it's sort of like an index), look up "self-control" and count how many verses use those exact words.

A wise man keeps himself under control. He keeps his lungs and his tongue under control. He keeps his fists under control. He deals with tough circumstances without hurting others.

How do you act when you get angry? What are some healthy ways to respond?

DAY 13

KEEPING A CLEAR CONSCIENCE

I strive always to keep my conscience clear before God and man.

ACTS 24:16

God has given everybody on earth a conscience. It's part of the package. A conscience is your mind knowing the difference between right and wrong. When you do wrong, your conscience makes you feel bad. When you do what's right, you have peace. The apostle Paul said he tried to keep a clear conscience by doing what was right before God and before people.

If you think that a conscience is a tiny angel fluttering at your right ear telling you to do good, and a tiny devil at your left ear tempting you to lie or take another cookie, you've been watching way too much TV. A conscience is the knowledge that certain things are right and certain things are wrong. For example, your conscience tells you that caring for the weak is right and honoring your parents is right, but stealing is wrong. When you're tempted to do wrong, your conscience reminds you that it's wrong. If you go ahead and do it anyway, your conscience kicks in again, making you feel guilty. If you apologize to the person you wronged, then you have a clear conscience again. And guess what? If you have a clear conscience and obey God's commands, you can be confident that God will answer your prayers. (See 1 John 3:21–22.) That's one of the benefits of having a clear conscience!

Your conscience is a gift from God. Don't ignore it. When it tells you to do something good, obey it. When your conscience tells you not to do something bad, well, duh, don't.

How can you keep a clear conscience? Is there a sin you need to confess or someone you need to apologize to?

DAY 14

RESISTING PEER PRESSURE

Do not follow the crowd in doing wrong. When you give testimony in a lawsuit, do not pervert justice by siding with the crowd.

EXODUS 23:2

In ancient Israel, when someone hurt someone else or caused an accident, or somebody's property was stolen or damaged, people took the matter before a judge. And back then, like today, people often argued for their friends. If you were a witness, they might pressure you to twist the truth to keep their friend out of trouble. The Bible called that "perverting justice."

Crowds aren't always wrong. Sometimes they're fun, like if you're playing soccer or enjoying yourself at a carnival. But there are times when you need to break away from the herd. If a group of guys starts lying about some kid to get him in trouble or want him to get all the blame for some fight when it was only partly his fault, don't go along with it—even if they tell you, "He has it coming."

Why go with the crowd just to be accepted? Who needs friends who act like that? Of course, sometimes kids will say that if you don't go along with them they'll get you in trouble. That's when it takes guts to do the right thing and to refuse to lie. Eventually liars will be found out, and when they are, you'll be glad you didn't go along with them.

Don't side with kids if they're setting somebody up. Tell the truth, even if it makes you unpopular. It's a sign you are becoming a mature Christian.

Have you ever broken away from a crowd? If so, what happened?

DAY 15

BEEFING UP YOUR BRAIN POWER

To these four young men God gave knowledge and understanding of all kinds of literature and learning.

DANIEL 1:17

King Nebuchadnezzar wanted some new servants, so he told his man Ashpenaz to pick youth who were good at learning and quick to understand. Ashpenaz tapped Daniel and his friends, gave them a crash course in Babylonian, plopped big stacks of literature in front of them, and said, "Here, learn this." Sure, Daniel and pals were smart, but they were overwhelmed. So they prayed, and God helped their brains learn even better than they normally did.

Maybe you're naturally smart: Your dad's a rocket scientist and your mom's a nuclear physicist, so of course you were born with a beefed-up brain. But what happens when you need to learn stuff that's way over your head? Sure, you can do some extra studying, but even smart kids burn out. And hey, let's be real: Chances are good that your parents aren't rocket scientists or nuclear physicists, and you're about average in the brains department. What then?

Do what you can do: Pay attention in class and study hard. Those things are huge. But if you don't want your brain to wear out like an overused eraser, pray for extra ability to understand. Need wisdom and knowledge? James 1:5 says, "If any of you lacks wisdom, you should ask God, who gives generously to all." That's a promise! But you gotta ask.

Remember, God's not limited to helping you with just the stuff you're naturally good at. God helped Daniel and his friends with "all kinds of learning."

How do you respond when you come up against a challenge? Name a couple of ways you can turn to God for help.

DAY 16

HOW WE GOT THE BIBLE

"How did you come to write all this? Did Jeremiah dictate it?" "Yes," Baruch replied, "he dictated all these words to me, and I wrote them in ink on the scroll."

JEREMIAH 36:17-18

How did we get the Bible? The words in the Bible were inspired by God. In some cases, God spoke directly to prophets who wrote down his words. And Jeremiah spent forty years repeating God's exact words to his scribe Baruch and the people of Judah. Jeremiah was even put into jail for the difficult news he spoke, but he continued to repeat God's message. And later in ancient Israel, flocks of scribes had the job of making exact copies of the prophets' books. Today, thanks to those scribes, we have a reliable record of God's Word.

Has a teacher ever given you a complicated explanation that you didn't write down? Then when you tried to remember it later, you forgot it completely, remembered only a word or two, or got it totally mixed up. And memory loss even hits with short, simple messages! Think how many times you say to your mom, "Yeah, I'll do it," but a minute later whatever she said is totally wiped out of your mind.

That's why God had his prophets write down what he said right away. God inspired many prophets and writers because he wanted to be sure that people knew what he was telling them. So, people like you, living today, know exactly what he wants you to do.

Thank God for ink and scrolls and paper! Thank God for prophets and scribes who knew how to write! Thank God that these words have been preserved and delivered to us. That's how we got the Bible.

Why is reading and obeying the Bible an important part of being a Christian?

DAY 17

LEARNING FROM THE MASTER TEACHER

When they saw the courage of Peter and John and realized that they were unschooled, ordinary men, they were astonished and they took note that these men had been with Jesus.

ACTS 4:13

Peter and John were telling the crowds about Jesus when the temple guards snagged them and dragged them before the top religious council. Now, the religious rulers could see that Peter and John were just regular guys. They were rough-and-tumble, working-class guys and hadn't received higher education, yet these boys were so sure of the facts and so bold declaring them, it was clear they'd been with the master teacher, Jesus.

Now, like Peter and John, you are probably a regular guy—you try to do your best, and there is something you are really good at. Maybe you aren't pulling an A+ in math, but you love to read. Maybe you're good at designing and creating art. Maybe you are very generous with your friends. Maybe there is something that makes you stand out in a crowd. Most likely, you have your strengths and your weaknesses, and you blend in with average people.

If you know Jesus and you know the Bible, you're not just one more average person. If you know the Man, then you know the truly important things about life, and you can't help but stand out. Get close to Jesus and it will show! Other people can't help but notice something different about you.

It's important to be smart about science and math and other stuff, but it's most important of all to have a relationship with Jesus.

How would you describe your relationship with Jesus? What can you do to draw closer to him?

DAY 18

GIRLS ARE COOL

There is neither . . . male nor female, for you are all one in Christ Jesus.

GALATIANS 3:28

Many ancient peoples—including Israelites—looked down on women. That's the way it was back then. In ancient days, a woman's word really didn't count. She couldn't even be a witness in a court case. When Jesus came along, he put that attitude out on the curb with the trash. Instead of putting women down, Jesus showed the world how important they were. Did you know that the very first people to witness that he had been raised from the dead were women? It's true!

In today's verse, Paul is saying that we can't judge people by whether they're male or female. Now, that doesn't mean that men and women are the same. They're different, to be sure, but men are not better than women. They're equal. Yet even today some boys think they're cooler than girls. They say stuff like, "Boys rule, girls drool." Listen guys: Babies drool, Jesus rules, and both boys and girls are cool.

No sweat if you'd rather hang out with guys than girls. Boys are interested in boy stuff, so that's perfectly normal. But the thing is, you've got to treat girls with respect. That doesn't mean you need to like all the things that girls like; no one's asking you to paint your fingernails. Let girls do girl stuff. That's their thing. Just don't look down on them for it.

Girls are different than boys—no one's arguing with that—but Jesus loves both guys and gals the same! That's the bottom line.

What are some practical ways you can treat the females in your life with respect?

DAY 19

RESPECTING THE ELDERLY

Stand up in the presence of the aged, show respect for the elderly and revere your God.

LEVITICUS 19:32

This wasn't just an ancient Israelite custom. Once upon a time even in America, if you were sitting when an elderly man or woman entered the room, you stood up to greet him or her. You did it to honor the person. You also offered him or her your chair. An old man named Job was so respected that when he arrived at the meeting place, the other elders rose to their feet (Job 29:7–8). It was like getting a standing ovation.

What about today? If your grandparents are visiting, is your brain riveted to what they might be planning to give you? Or do you respect them even if they don't lead in camels loaded down with presents?

We should respect older people, and there are lots of ways

to do this: One of the most important is to show them love and appreciation. Hugs work. Another way to show respect is to listen carefully when they speak and to answer their questions. If you want to show respect, don't pass them in the food line or do your wounded baboon imitation when they're trying to rest.

One of the cool things about honoring and respecting the elderly is that you're also honoring God because you're treating the elderly the way he wants them to be treated.

Why is it important to show respect to people who are older than you?

ONE OF THE COOL THINGS ABOUT HONORING AND RESPECTING THE ELDERLY IS THAT YOU'RE ALSO HONORING GOD BECAUSE YOU'RE TREATING THE ELDERLY THE WAY HE WANTS THEM TO BE TREATED.

DAY 20

A FAITHFUL FRIEND

What a person desires is unfailing love . . . Many claim to have unfailing love, but a faithful person who can find?

PROVERBS 19:22; 20:6

When the Bible says that people want unfailing love, it's not talking about mushy romantic love. What it means is that we want friends we can totally count on. If a friend says he'll help overhaul a car engine, we like it when the guy shows up. We dislike it when the guy doesn't. We aren't happy if someone's our friend one day but not talking to us the next.

Guys have emotions, true, and if your buddy made a joke about you and you were offended instead of finding it ha-ha funny, you really won't feel like keeping your word and helping him do stuff. So what do you do? Find a way to punish him? Deliberately let him down when he needs your help the most? If you don't care about a friend, yeah, it's tempting.

But if you really have "unfailing love" and aren't just saying that you do, then you're not faithful one day and unfaithful the next. Sure, you tell the guy that you think he was a jerk, but you stay friends. You can't just claim you'll stand by him through thick and thin. You have to actually do it, even when he's acting thick and your patience is thin.

If you're someone's best bud and you tell him, "You can count on me," then you have to be faithful and be there when you said you would.

What are some qualities that you appreciate in a good friend? Do you bring those positive qualities to your friendships?

DAY 21

YOUR NEIGHBOR'S TOYS

You shall not covet . . . anything that belongs to your neighbor.

EXODUS 20:17

People have a right to their belongings, so God wrote about this in the Ten Commandments. Rule number eight says not to take anything that doesn't belong to you. Then, for good measure, God added rule number ten that says not to even covet anything that doesn't belong to you. (To "covet" means to be upset that someone else owns something we feel we deserve.)

If we want something in the store and we have the money to buy it, good for us. If we're saving our money to buy what we want, way to go. But the problem comes when we want something that belongs to our neighbor, but he or she isn't selling. When we're drooling over someone else's stuff, two things are happening: one, we're not content with what we have, and two, we might start dreaming up ways to get that person's stuff.

The best way to avoid coveting something that belongs to someone else is to first be thankful for what we have. Chances are we want what the other guy has but really don't need it. The second way to avoid coveting is to thank God that the other guy has what he has. You can be happy for someone else, right?

God put laws in the Bible to protect people's belongings because he wants us to keep our hands off them. He doesn't even want us to give other people's things the greedy eyeball.

What types of things are you most likely to covet? How can you guard yourself against coveting those types of things?

DAY 22

GO WHERE YOU MEAN TO GO

Do not conform to the pattern of this world, but be transformed by the renewing of your mind.

ROMANS 12:2

If you're a Christian, you're a changed person. Once Jesus has saved you, your old ways of thinking begin to get replaced. God sends his Spirit into your heart and starts changing you by giving your mind a new outlook. He knows you'll be tempted to flip back to acting like those who haven't been changed by Jesus, so he warns, "From now on don't conform to your old ways."

Have you ever started to go somewhere in your house and then been distracted? You hop off your bed, walk down the hall, and . . . wander into the kitchen. You look around and wonder, "Huh? Why did I come here?" You weren't even hungry, but you just walked to Grand Snack Central out of habit. You were following the old programming, the old pattern. If you want to go to where you really mean to go, you need to remember you have a new direction—then head there.

When God comes into your life, he begins changing you immediately. You go to do something stupid and you realize, "Whoa! I don't want to do that anymore!" So you stop. Sometimes the changes are big and fast. Other times it takes a while to stop mindlessly repeating old habits. It takes time to replace old habits with new habits.

It can be easy to flip back to your old way of thinking. So make an effort to stop that and to let God's Spirit transform your thought patterns.

Name some ways being a Christian changes you.

DAY 23

WHY GOD GIVES US GIFTS

There are different kinds of gifts, but the same Spirit. . . . Now to each one the manifestation of the Spirit is given for the common good.

1 CORINTHIANS 12:4, 7

When the Spirit of God lives in your heart, he gives you power to live the Christian faith. But he also gives you some unique "gifts." These gifts are abilities and spiritual talents, and they're different for each person. But the reason is always the same—to help you and others.

Ever wanted to have special powers—like miraculous powers? Well, we humans can't do miracles. But God can! Sometimes he gives people gifts of insight, knowledge, or ability. If that happens, it's not some power you have. God's Spirit is the one who does it. If you could do it on demand, you'd be tempted to use it for selfish reasons . . . like kids in the movies do.

God's Spirit gives Christians all kinds of spiritual gifts. Sometimes he gives believers the gift of knowing what others are going through so they can pray for them or encourage them. Maybe God will give you the gift of wisdom or the gift of knowledge. You'll know something that you had no way of finding out. Or maybe your spiritual gift will be something totally different. It might take time for your gift to show up, but it will show up.

Just remember: God doesn't let you do cool stuff to make you look great. That's not the way God operates. He does it to help you and to help others.

Write down some of the ways that God has gifted you. How can you use those gifts to serve others?

DAY 24

MIXING AND MINGLING

I now realize how true it is that God does not show favoritism but accepts from every nation the one who fears him and does what is right.

ACTS 10:34-35

The apostle Peter was visiting a Roman named Cornelius, and at first Peter felt pretty uncomfortable going to his home. As Peter told Cornelius, "It is against our law for a Jew to associate with a Gentile or visit him" (Acts 10:28). Actually, it wasn't against God's law. God only said that Jews shouldn't worship idols and shouldn't marry Gentiles (non-Jews) who worshiped idols. It didn't say they should refuse to even visit them.

God showed Peter that God doesn't play favorites with any race. The Jews weren't better than all other people in the world who loved God. Peter realized this two thousand years ago, yet some people today still haven't clued in. They feel it's somehow not "right" for people of different races to mix and mingle. They don't associate with people who aren't just like them. Why? Because it's just, well . . . it's just not done.

But if someone loves God and is living for the truth, God accepts him and you should too. A person's race is not a qualification for being chosen by God. Sure, that kid may look different, speak differently, and eat different food, but don't let those things stop you from accepting him. It's time to realize that some of our customs are not God's idea but are the prejudices of humans.

God loves everyone, so don't judge someone just because he's different. If he loves and obeys Jesus, he's your brother.

How is racism a sin against God and other people?

DAY 25

IN TRAINING

Everyone who competes in the games goes into strict training.

1 CORINTHIANS 9:25

The apostle Paul lived in the city of Corinth for two years, and after he left he wrote to the Christians there. Now, a funny thing, often when Paul explained spiritual things to them, he used the language of training for athletic competitions. Why? Because Corinthians were passionate sports fans. Corinthians not only trained for the Olympic Games every four years, they also hosted the Isthmian games every two years. And the Christians there went wild in the stands like everybody else.

You still need to train for competitions today. Whether you're into basketball, hockey, or martial arts, it takes dedication and focus to become good at it. It helps if you absolutely love the sport, because all that repetition can get boring at times. You also have to know the game's rules. Like them or not, that's how the game is played, so your coach makes you learn them by heart and makes sure you follow them.

Today, just as in Paul's day, Christian life is like athletic training. You need to be as wild about Christ as the Corinthians were about their sports events. When you're passionate about something, it's easy to be devoted to it. And when you're devoted to something, you accept the repetitive training and strict rules as part of the package.

Stay passionate, stay focused, and all the rest will follow. That's true both in sports and in being a Christian.

What are some similarities between being a Christian and being an athlete?

DAY 26

ON YOUR MARK, GET SET, GO!

The beginning of the good news about Jesus the Messiah, the Son of God.

MARK 1:1

There are four Gospels in the Bible—Matthew, Mark, Luke, and John. But here's an interesting point about the Gospel of Mark: Bible scholars believe that Gospel was originally written for the Romans. The Romans loved action, so Mark included mostly action in his book and hardly any parables or sermons or prayers.

Your youth leader just told you to read the Bible. Your dad agrees. Your mom says there is lots of good stuff for you to learn about. Ready? Set? But where do you start? It can be pretty overwhelming!

Maybe you think it would be best to just flip it open and read whatever you point to first. So you turn to Leviticus 13:47

and read, "As for any fabric that is spoiled with a defiling mold—any woolen or linen clothing." You close your Bible and then open it to 1 Chronicles 1:40 and read, "The sons of Shobal: Alvan, Manahath, Ebal, Shepho and Onam. The sons of Zibeon: Aiah and Anah." You close your Bible again, and by now you're probably ready to keep it closed and go watch TV.

Listen guys, start with the Gospels. And if you really want a high-energy read, start with the Gospel of Mark. When Mark talks about what Jesus did, he uses a lot of fast-paced words like "immediately," "at once," and "quickly." Mark also describes the action in colorful detail. That makes it a great book for boys. If you've never read any Gospel story from beginning to end, start reading Mark today.

What types of things would you like to learn about Jesus from reading the Gospels?

DAY 27

BEING BORN AGAIN

Jesus replied, "Very truly I tell you, no one can see the kingdom of God unless they are born again."

JOHN 3:3

Ever wonder where the term "born again" came from? One night an old, white-bearded teacher named Nicodemus came to Jesus. Nick nearly fell over backward when Jesus told him that the only way to enter God's kingdom was to be born again. Nick asked if Jesus meant he had to enter a second time into his mother's womb to be born. Jesus explained, "Flesh gives birth to flesh, but the Spirit gives birth to spirit" (John 3:6).

See, you've already been born physically. A physical birth lands you in this world, screaming your lungs out. That's what the cake and candles and presents are all about each year. That's a good start, but it isn't enough. You also need to be born spiritually. You may ask, "But how do I do that? How do I become born again?"

Here's how it happens: When you believe in Jesus, the

Holy Spirit enters your heart to give life to your spirit. God's Spirit gives you life—eternal life, in fact—and you've just been born again! You've become one of God's own kids. Sound terrific? Why would God do such a fantastic thing? He does it because he loves you.

Do you want to live forever in God's kingdom? Pray for Jesus to forgive you and ask the Holy Spirit to come into your heart. Then you'll have eternal life. That's what being born again is about.

In your own words, describe what it means to be "born again."

DAY 28

SETTLING DISAGREEMENTS

Let's not have any quarreling between you and me . . . If you go to the left, I'll go to the right; if you go to the right, I'll go to the left.

GENESIS 13:8-9

You don't always have to have your way. Let others have first choice sometimes. This scripture comes from a famous story in the Bible that reminds us of this principle. Abraham and his nephew Lot both owned tons of sheep and goats, but the place they were at had little pasture and few watering holes. Soon Abe and Lot's herdsmen began fighting. So Abraham took Lot up to the top of a hill, showed him the entire country, and said, "You choose first. I'll take what you don't want."

Lot naturally picked the best pastures and left the drier land for Abraham. But Abe didn't mind, and afterwards God mightily blessed him. Now, you may wonder, is this example relevant when your little brother wants to play with the X-box, leaving you the old toys? Does it apply when your sister wants to watch one movie and you want to watch another?

Yes, this principle applies. When you settle disagreements, be fair and generous. Now, this doesn't mean giving everything away nor always letting others go first forever and ever, all the time, every time. But it does mean letting them choose first sometimes.

Being fair means being fair to all people. You'll try your best to be fair if you care for the other person—and a man of God should care for others.

How do you act when things don't go your way? What is the best way to respond?

DAY 29

MAGIC BOOKS DISAPPEAR

A number who had practiced sorcery brought their scrolls together and burned them publicly.

ACTS 19:19

The apostle Paul spent a couple years in Ephesus. This city was a center for witches and sorcerers and magicians. Then lots of these guys became Christians and decided to burn their "spell" books. They torched 50,000 drachmas' worth! Since a drachma is worth about a day's wages, that's a lot of abracadabras going up in smoke! (Poof! Watch me make these magic books disappear!) These guys were serious about cleaning the junk out of their lives.

Today there are tons of spell books and movies around. We're not talking about Merlin or other fantasy stories about magic. We're talking about the old pagan religion of witchcraft itself. People read the witchy books because they're interested in secret wisdom and figure these books have it. Not smart. Or they figure that by mumbling magical rhymes they'll get quick answers to problems. Not. It's just bad poetry.

If you really want wisdom, plug into the one true God—not the false goat-god of witchcraft. Our God has the answers. He also has the power to give genuine answers to prayer. His miracles may take a while to happen, but they're worth waiting for. Best of all, faith in Jesus gives you eternal life in heaven, something witchcraft can never do. Take a tip from the ancient sorcerers of Ephesus! When they found new life in Jesus, they gladly burned all their old spell books! They didn't care how much it cost them.

Why is it wrong for Christians to participate in witchcraft and sorcery?

DAY 30

BATTLE LOST TO THE BOTTLE

Ben-Hadad and the 32 kings allied with him were in their tents getting drunk.

1 KINGS 20:16

It's a bad idea to be sitting around anytime getting drunk as skunks, but this was a particularly bad time for Ben-Hadad, king of the Arameans. At this very moment, the army of Israel was marching out to fight Ben-Hadad's army. The Israelites were hugely outnumbered, but at least they were sober. Ben-Hadad's army was ready to fight, but the problem was that Ben and the thirty-two wino-kings were so smashed they couldn't lead the battle—so their armies lost.

Alcohol still causes huge losses these days. Talk about wasted finances! Some guys spend thousands of dollars a year on booze. Alcoholism can wreck a successful career, make a mess of a marriage, and break up a family. Drunk driving causes many deaths, and—sad to say—quite a few drunk drivers are teens. What are teens doing drinking?

Alcoholism is a huge problem in America today, so don't you be the next casualty. Don't experiment with liquor no matter how much the other kids tease. Just say no to the bottle and mean it. Come to think of it, don't even hang around with kids who abuse alcohol. They'll constantly be pressuring you to start drinking, and who needs that?

You have your whole life ahead of you. Make the most of it. Don't blow the whole thing like Ben-Hadad and his drinking buddies who lost the battle to the bottle.

Make a list of several good reasons to avoid alcohol.

DAY 31

REALLY LEARNING

. . . Always learning but never able to come to a knowledge of the truth.

2 TIMOTHY 3:7

Back in Paul's day, some people were like Curious George—constantly interested in new stuff without thinking about the big picture. They gathered knowledge nonstop, but all their scattered education did was fill up their minds with scraps of information. They still didn't acknowledge the truth, meaning they knew all about the truth, but they hadn't let it change their lives. They were like squirrels storing away nuts they never ate.

It's the same today with some kids raised in Christian homes: They know all about the Bible and Jesus dying on the cross, but they've never given their hearts to him. Other kids have taken that step—and that's a terrific start—but then slacked off on living as a Christian. They learn about the Bible, but it seems like just a collection of interesting stories about talking donkeys and battles and Noah building an ark and yada yada.

It's great to learn more about the Bible, but the most important thing is to know Jesus and to live your life so that it really counts! Don't just read the Bible, but accept it and let it change your life. When you actually acknowledge the truth, it hits you between the eyes: The Bible's about a life-changing relationship with God. The interesting stories are just pepperoni on the pizza.

It's cool to learn about all the bits and pieces, but don't miss the big picture. Get an actual knowledge of the truth, and then keep learning!

Write down a few things that you've learned from reading the Bible. How can you obey those truths in your own life?

DAY 32

WHY WE WORSHIP GOD

To him who loves us and has freed us from our sins by his blood . . . to him be glory and power for ever and ever!

REVELATION 1:5-6

Why does the Bible tell us to worship God? Does God have an ego problem? Does he need people to constantly repeat how great he is? No. Worship simply means recognizing how awesome God is—and saying it. We worship Jesus because he's God's Son, and he loved us enough to die for us and was powerful enough to return to life. Does Jesus get proud when we praise him? No. He said, "I am gentle and humble in heart" (Matthew 11:29).

Imagine your dad works in the Air Force, and one day he gives you high-level clearance and takes you into the super-secret hangar of the newest experimental jet. (You wish!) You walk in and there's this shimmering, monstrous, powerful thing! Your eyes bug out and you shout, "Whoa! Awesome!" Some things are jaw-dropping awesome.

God is far, far more powerful and awesome than that, and his Holy Spirit packs way more power! And what Jesus did by dying to save us and then coming back to life deserves our praise! Is Jesus glorious? Yes. Is Jesus powerful? You bet he is. So when we worship God, we're simply recognizing how fantastic he is.

When you realize how awesome God is and what fantastic things he has done for you, and you're in awe and feeling grateful—that's worship.

What types of things motivate you to worship God?

DAY 33

HAVE MERCY—FORGIVE OTHERS

But if you do not forgive others their sins, your Father will not forgive your sins.

MATTHEW 6:15

Once a guy owed a king millions of dollars, so the king ordered that he, his family, and everything he owned be sold to pay the debt. The man begged for mercy, so the king forgave the whole debt. Then that guy found a fellow who owed him a few bucks and demanded he pay. The fellow begged for mercy, but the first guy threw him in prison. The king was furious. He asked, "Shouldn't you have had mercy on your fellow servant just as I had on you?" (Matthew 18:21–33).

If you're like most kids, you've broken quite a few of God's commandments—sometimes day after day. But if you accept that Jesus died on the cross for your sins and ask God to forgive you, you're forgiven. God doesn't hold your sins against you. So then what do you do when your brother accidentally breaks your Lego model? Punch him? Tell him he's never allowed in your room again?

The point of Jesus' parable is this: God has been merciful to us and has forgiven us for many sins, so we need to turn around and be merciful to those who sin against us. If we don't forgive others when they offend or hurt us, God won't forgive us our sins. He may let us suffer the consequences of our mistakes to teach us a lesson.

God prefers to forgive. He'd rather not discipline you. So be merciful to others, just like God has been merciful to you.

List some ways you can be merciful and forgiving to your family and friends.

DAY 34

DON'T JUST WAIL! PRAY!

They were at their wits' end. Then they cried out to the Lord in their trouble, and he brought them out of their distress.

PSALM 107:27-28

One day a merchant ship was sailing along when a terrible storm hit. Monster waves lifted the ship high into the sky, then hurled it down into the depths. Then up again, then down again. The storm was so wild, the sailors staggered around the deck like drunken men. They were out of their minds with fear. They began praying! Oh yeah, they prayed! And God answered. He stilled the storm to a whisper, and they reached port safe and sound.

Have you ever been at your wits' end? Maybe you're not staggering and sliding all over the deck of a ship, but have you ever been in danger? Have you ever been afraid? What do you do? Do you cry out to God?

God says, "You will seek me and find me when you seek me with all your heart" (Jeremiah 29:13). That's a promise. Only make sure you're actually praying with all your heart and not just lying on your bed moaning and wailing. God said about the ancient Israelites, "They do not cry out to me from their hearts but wail on their beds" (Hosea 7:14).

When you're at your wits' end, don't just wail. Cry out to God. He'll deliver you. He'll help you when no one else can, but it might not be in the way you expect.

What situations tend to make you feel overwhelmed or "at your wits' end"? Next time you feel that way, how can you remind yourself to pray instead of panic?

DAY 35

EATING AWAY YOUR PEACE OF MIND

Do not be anxious about anything, but in everything, by prayer and petition, with thanksgiving, present your requests to God.

PHILIPPIANS 4:6

When the Bible says don't be anxious, it means don't worry and be fearful. Worried thoughts nibble at the edge of your mind and eat up your peace, so God tells you flat out, "Don't worry about anything!" You know how your mom saves you a piece of cake for after school, but your little sister keeps going to the fridge and taking a little nibble here, a little nibble there, until by the time you get home, your entire piece of cake has been devoured? Worry devours your peace of mind like your sister devours that piece of cake. What kinds of things are you worried about? Your family's finances? A big test? Some kid who harasses you? Being late to a friend's house?

If you find yourself worrying or pacing or biting your nails, stop immediately! Drag that worry to God and pray about it—not just the big worries but the little ones too. God isn't going to groan even if you bring a piddly concern to him. After all, the Bible says, "Cast all your anxiety on him because he cares for you" (1 Peter 5:7). God cares about it all. (By the way, when the verse tells you to petition God, this is a one-person petition. You don't need a thousand signatures on your prayer before you present it to God. Just pray.) Don't let worry eat your peace of mind. God doesn't want you to worry. He cares for you, so hand your anxious thoughts over to him.

Write down three things you most often worry about. How can you make a habit each morning (or sometime during the day) to pray and hand these worries over to God?

DAY 36

DEFEAT YOUR GIANTS

You yourself heard then that the Anakites were there . . . but, the Lord helping me, I will drive them out.

JOSHUA 14:12

When the Israelites left Egypt for Canaan, Moses sent twelve spies ahead to check things out. Those guys came back shakin', saying that there were giants in the land—Anakites! No way could they conquer them! Only Caleb and Joshua believed they could. The unbelieving Israelites had to wander in the desert for forty years until a new generation was ready to invade Canaan. The giants were still waiting, but Caleb believed that—with God's help—he could tromp them. And he did.

Are there giants in your life stopping you from entering your promised land? Do huge doubts make you afraid to try out for a sports team? Are you afraid to be downstairs alone? Do you worry that some giant monster is hiding in a closet?

Does it seem like way too much work to finish your science project?

Listen. If God wants you to do something, then you can overcome the giants in the way—no matter how big they are. Whether you're staring at a nine-foot-tall Anakite or facing your worst fears, God can help you. You can jerk open that closet door or try out for that team or put together a huge science display—whatever.

God helped Caleb defeat the giants when others didn't have the faith for it. Your problem may be too gigantic for you alone, but it's not too big for you and God together.

Name an obstacle you'd like to overcome. Pause a moment and ask God to help you.

DAY 37

UNDER PRESSURE

We were under great pressure, far beyond our ability to endure.

2 CORINTHIANS 1:8

The apostle Paul had it so tough in the city of Ephesus, he said he was like a gladiator doing hand-to-hand combat with lions in the arena (1 Corinthians 15:32). Paul was under intense pressure! Sometimes he doubted he'd even survive. Did he go down? No. When troubles hit, he prayed and depended on God more than ever, and God helped him make it.

You know how you feel when your homework or a project comes crashing down on top of you like a tidal wave? You're so overwhelmed that you throw up your hands and groan, "It's impossible!" You probably whine too, but we won't go there. Or you know how wide your mouth hangs open when your dad takes you to the garage on a sunny Saturday and tells you that you have till dinner to finish cleaning it? You get that "gladiator against the lions" feeling.

You only have so much strength, and sometimes you'll be in situations that are far bigger than you can handle yourself. Or at least you'll feel that the task is so huge that you can't do it. Well, God wants you to learn to depend on his strength, not just on your limited strength.

When you feel you can't do a job—it's too big or too difficult—know that with God helping you, you can make it.

Describe a time when God helped you get through a hard situation. What happened?

DAY 38

QUALITY RESEARCH

Since I myself have carefully investigated everything from the beginning, I too decided to write an orderly account for you.

LUKE 1:3

Luke was a physician living in Greece. It had been almost thirty years since Jesus had been crucified and raised from the dead, and Luke wanted to write a gospel for Greek Christians. He didn't want to do a sloppy job, either. He wanted to see the places where things had happened and interview eyewitnesses. So Luke sailed all the way to Israel to investigate the facts. He then wrote an orderly account, meaning an organized, easy-to-understand, and reliable report.

What about you? When your teacher tells you to write a report on something, do you check things out on the ground, investigate on the Internet, and interview people who know about it? Do you check your facts carefully, or do you slide by with as little work as possible—just enough to pass? Or if your mom wants to know who's responsible for making a mess, do you check the facts carefully before blaming someone? Do people know they can trust you as a source of reliable information?

The kind of careful research Luke did stands the test of time. You can be sure that your faith is built upon the truth because Luke double-checked and triple-checked his information. So take care with your research. Make sure it's not only accurate, but that people can easily understand it. This is true for schoolwork as well as telling others the facts about Jesus.

When it comes to investigating facts and explaining them simply, Luke stands out as a top researcher and an example to follow.

Why is it important to be accurate and get your facts correct?

DAY 39

CONTROLLING YOUR THOUGHTS

We take captive every thought to make it obedient to Christ.

2 CORINTHIANS 10:5

Jesus said that you should not only worship God with all your heart, but that you should worship him with your whole mind (Matthew 22:37). But how can you do that if your mind's running all over the place? You have to gather your thoughts. You have to capture them and make them obedient to Christ. The Greek word for captive in this verse means "to take prisoner." Picture prisoners marching along in chains and someone's poking them, saying, "Okaaay, boys, keep moving."

Would you say your thoughts are under control? Or is your brain more like a zoo where every single monkey has broken out of its cage and is swinging all over the place, screaming and going bananas? Example: If you're a Christian, you know you're supposed to forgive others. But if someone crosses you, does your mind plan a hundred ways to hang him up by his toes?

No matter how wild an imagination you were born with, you don't need to let it take you on a mental roller-coaster ride. Maybe you're spacey or creative, but that's not a reason to give your mind an all-day pass to the amusement park. You can control your thoughts, but you have to be militant about it. You have to be aggressive.

You don't want to end up brain-dead from all the confusion, so forget the saying "Take no prisoners." Take your thoughts prisoner. Take as many prisoners as you can. Then put those captive thoughts to work for Jesus.

Name a couple of ways in which you would like to improve your thoughts. Do you struggle with worry, thoughts of revenge, or anxiety?

DAY 40

FOUR KEYS OF FRIENDSHIP

Remind the people . . . to slander no one, to be peaceable and considerate, and always be gentle toward everyone.

TITUS 3:2

Paul's advice to Christians is: (1) slander no one (in other words, no mean-spirited trash talking); (2) be peaceable (don't bulldoze others by trying to push for what we want); (3) be considerate (duh); and (4) be humble (don't think that we're better than others).

These rules were written to help Christians stay out of trouble with the law, but they're also great advice on how to treat and keep friends. Have you ever noticed how obnoxious, angry kids lose friends by treating them badly?

Okay, so it's clear that people don't like to be slandered and bad-mouthed. And it's also obvious that if we don't insist on our way, but compromise and work things out, people enjoy having us around. And of course, being considerate of others is important. But why is humility a big deal? It's important because if we don't have proud attitudes, we won't end up arguing so much, or putting others down.

God wants us to treat others well because he cares for how they feel. It just so happens that acting like a Christian is also a great way to make and keep friends.

Glance back at Paul's four pieces of advice. Which one of these areas would you like to work on?

GOD WANTS US TO TREAT OTHERS WELL BECAUSE HE CARES FOR HOW THEY FEEL. IT JUST SO HAPPENS THAT ACTING LIKE A CHRISTIAN IS ALSO A GREAT WAY TO MAKE AND KEEP FRIENDS.

DAY 41

JESUS' POWER OVER DEMONS

When he saw Jesus, he cried out and fell at his feet, shouting at the top of his voice, "What do you want with me, Jesus, Son of the Most High God? I beg you, don't torture me!"

LUKE 8:28

A long time ago in Israel, a demon-possessed madman lived in a graveyard beside the Sea of Galilee. Then Jesus' boat landed. When the Son of God stepped ashore, the guy rushed out from the tombs to meet him. One look at Jesus, and the demons inside this guy went bonkers. The guy fell down and began screaming at the top of his voice to Jesus, "I beg you, don't torture me!" Right away Jesus cast the devils out of him.

Some movies and comic books have things totally backward. They describe demons and evil spirits as mighty, fearsome beings—which some of them are—but the way they have it, it's usually only some bigger demon who can finally beat them. Modern comic and movie scriptwriters have totally forgotten what the Bible says.

When Jesus met demons, the demons trembled with terror, flopped to the ground, and wailed and begged him not to punish them. When the Son of God looked them in the eyes, they screamed and shrieked and went crazy with fear.

So who's the most powerful? Jesus! You don't have to be afraid of the devil or demons because this same powerful Jesus is still protecting us today.

Why is it important to be aware that Jesus is more powerful than the devil?

DAY 42

MIRACLES ARE EVIDENCE

Now while he was in Jerusalem . . . many people saw the signs he was doing and believed in his name.

JOHN 2:23

When you read the story of Jesus' life, one thing that jumps out at you is how many miracles he did. People who saw these things were astonished. This man was clearly no ordinary man, and many people believed that he was the Son of God. In fact, Jesus' enemies complained, "Here is this man performing many miraculous signs. If we let him go on like this, everyone will believe in him." They knew that miracles were strong evidence that Jesus had divine power.

And miracles didn't only happen in Bible days. God still answers prayers when Christians pray to him in Jesus' name. He still does miracles today: big ones that make you go "Wow!" and small everyday ones. Stop and think about some prayer

God answered for your family. You've probably even forgotten some of them. Ask your parents or grandparents to remind you.

People pray for lots of little things every day, and time and again God answers! The problem is that by the time God answers the prayer, people have often forgotten that they prayed for it. We don't always recognize when God does something for us. You know how you take it for granted when your mom and dad do things for you? Well, God does lots of stuff for you too. So pay attention and thank him whenever you can.

Jesus did miracles, and those miracles proved his love and power. Although he isn't walking around on earth today, his power to do miracles is still here. He still answers our prayers today.

Can you think of a time when God answered a prayer for you or your family? What happened?

DAY 43

PUTTING ON THE ARMOR OF LIGHT

The night is nearly over; the day is almost here. So let us put aside the deeds of darkness and put on the armor of light.

ROMANS 13:12

Obeying the Word of God is like waking up and getting dressed. When this verse says "the night is nearly over," it means that the world's present evil age has almost ended.

"The day is almost here" means Jesus is coming soon. It's time to get dressed. But remember, in order to put on the armor of light, you first have to put aside the deeds of darkness. Wake up and stop doing things that displease God.

You've seen those cartoon shows where heroes of the future prepare for battle. All they do is think *Armor on*, and suddenly these plates of shining armor begin whipping out of nowhere and snap in place all over their bodies. Within seconds they're covered. Maybe you wish you could dress like that in the morning, instead of struggling to button your shirt when you're half-asleep—then finding that you buttoned it wrong.

God's armor is the most fantastic kind of battle armor. You pray for his Spirit to cover you with all the pieces of his armor, and he does. But you also need to grab the weapons he gives, like the Sword of the Spirit. You won't be able to see these things with your eyes though. God's armor is armor of light, all right, but spiritual light. (Read all about it in Ephesians 6:10–17.)

You want to be one of God's warriors? Then ditch the deeds of darkness, put on the armor of light, and get serious about being one of his fighters.

Look up Ephesians 6:10-17 in your Bible. What is your favorite part of God's armor described in these verses?

DAY 44

HELPING YOUR FAITH GROW

Faith comes from hearing the message, and the message is heard through the word about Christ.

ROMANS 10:17

When you read the Gospels or hear your pastor talk about Jesus and God's Spirit opens your eyes to all the amazing stuff Jesus said and did, you just know that Jesus was one of a kind. No one else taught the amazing things he taught or did the miracles he did. And certainly no one else died and came back to life! And once you put your faith in Jesus and trust him to save you, you have eternal life.

But even after you believe in Jesus, your faith is still tested. Like maybe you're confused or afraid. Or maybe you're going through a difficult time. Maybe everything seems hopeless and you just need some hope to hang onto so you don't sink in the "quicksand of gloom."

Where do you get your hope? What helps you believe that God is with you and that things will turn out?

You get that hope and inspiration the same way you received it in the first place—by listening to the truth about Jesus and by sitting down and opening up your Bible and reading it. Are you worried about some problem? Are you afraid? Do you wonder where God is when you need him? Do you feel mentally wiped out?

If you want your faith to grow stronger, read God's Word. That's where your spiritual strength comes from. Plug in to God and recharge your batteries today.

Why does reading the Bible make your faith stronger?

DAY 45

HIDING GOD'S WORD DOWN DEEP

I have hidden your word in my heart that I might not sin against you.

PSALM 119:11

When this verse talks about hiding God's Word in your heart, it doesn't mean stashing it somewhere so little kids can't find it. When it says to "hide" it, the verse means getting the Bible so deep down in your mind that it's almost part of you. And it's not only talking about memorizing Bible verses, but also about tuning in to them. Do that and you're a lot less likely to sin against God.

If you have to make a decision and wonder what to do, it sure makes it a lot easier if a verse from the Bible suddenly comes to mind, telling you exactly what God thinks of your plans, right? Since you don't always have a Bible handy, plant some verses in your mind. Get them deep in your heart. And how do you do that?

Well, just like you have to memorize multiplication tables or lines from a play, you should memorize important verses from the Bible. Some people only have to read a verse a few times and it sticks. Good for them! But most of us, if we want to write it onto our brain's hard drive, have to actually memorize it. Do that. Then the Holy Spirit can remind you of it when you need direction the most. If you can't remember what God's Word says, it's easy to sin and do wrong things. If you know what the Bible says, it's a whole lot easier to make the right choice.

Pick out a scripture that you really need right now and spend a few minutes each day committing it to memory.

DAY 46

BITING YOUR TONGUE

The prudent hold their tongue . . . Even fools are thought wise if they keep silent.

PROVERBS 10:19; 17:28

There are times—lots of times, in fact—when it's wise to hold your tongue. That doesn't mean grabbing your tongue with your hands—you can hold it just fine with your teeth. Teeth are practically made for the job. That's not hard for a wise person. But for a fool, trying to hang on to his tongue is like trying to stay on a rodeo bull.

Some kids never stop talking. Know anyone like that? It's fine to be a talker. Chatty people are fun to be around, but not if their mouth pours out a non-ending stream of foolish jokes and grossness. Some kids talk about things they shouldn't just to see how many laughs they can get—like if their little brother wet his bed and they tell all his friends.

It's fun to joke around, but you've got to know what to joke about and when to zip your lip. If you know how to do that, you're wise. In fact, considering how fools like to talk, people may even think a fool is wise if he keeps silent. Like, maybe his mouth was full of pizza and he couldn't talk, but at least he missed saying something stupid.

Know when to hold on to your tongue. It doesn't take a lot of brains to keep your mouth shut, but you've got to use the brains you have.

What are some negative things that can happen when you fail to hold your tongue?

DAY 47

JUNK TALK

Do not let any unwholesome talk come out of your mouths, but only what is helpful for building others up according to their needs.

EPHESIANS 4:29

The opposite of wholesome, healthy food is unwholesome food, or junk food. Well, the opposite of wholesome talk is junk talk. Want to know what that is? Think of some kid swearing, acting out-of-control foolish, or trash-talking someone else. That's what the Bible means when it says not to let unwholesome talk come out of your mouth.

Some people don't think before they speak. They just blab whatever pops into their mind—potty humor, sick jokes, or whatever. As long as it's good for a laugh, they don't care who they gross out. It doesn't matter if it builds someone up and encourages that person or knocks them down and discourages them. And sure enough, junk talk drags everyone down.

That's why it's smart to think before you speak. Ask yourself, "What does this person need to hear?" Then say those things. That doesn't mean pouring on false compliments. Just be careful what you say. If you don't care for something, look for something descriptive to say that isn't hurtful. Like if your grandmother asks what you think of her new hairdo, don't reply, "Weird! It looks like gray cotton candy." Just say, "It has nice curls." Or if your friend asks what you think of his drawing, stop yourself from blurting out, "It reeks." Tell him what parts you like and offer a suggestion if he needs it.

When you think of other people's feelings before you speak, that's wisdom kicking in. Sometimes you can't help it if foolish thoughts pop into your mind. Just don't let them come out of your mouth.

Can you remember a time when you were on the receiving end of hurtful words? What did you learn from that experience that can guide you when you speak to others?

WHEN YOU THINK OF OTHER PEOPLE'S FEELINGS BEFORE YOU SPEAK, THAT'S WISDOM KICKING IN.

DAY 48

LAST-MINUTE SCRAMBLE

Sluggards not plow in season; so at harvest time they look but find nothing.

PROVERBS 20:4

The ground in Israel was usually so hard and dry that plows could barely break it up. But every autumn rains softened the soil. That's when farmers were out with their oxen and plows, planting crops. Everyone except for sluggards, that is. Those lazy guys kept putting the job off. By the time they finally got around to it, the ground was getting hard again. They plowed and scattered seeds, sure, but come harvest (surprise, surprise!) no crop—or a very poor crop.

Sound familiar? Instead of doing your homework or school assignment when you're supposed to, do you put it off till the last possible minute or only remember it at bedtime? If it's due the next day, do you do a rushed, sloppy job and get a low grade? This is called procrastination. A procrastinator knows what he's supposed to do but doesn't want to do it, so he drags his feet until it becomes an all-out emergency.

It's easy to avoid that last-minute scramble: Do your homework when you're supposed to. Or if you're getting ready for school or church, stay focused on dressing, combing your hair, and finding your shoes. That way you can walk to the car instead of running there half-clothed and barefoot.

Don't be a sluggard. Roll up your sleeves and do your work when it's supposed to be done. Get it done and out of the way. Then go have your fun.

List some advantages of getting your tasks done on time or early.

DAY 49

BE HAPPY, YOUNG MAN

You who are young, be happy while you are young, and let your heart give you joy in the days of your youth.

ECCLESIASTES 11:9

Here's a command kids gotta love: Thou shalt have fun! It isn't exactly a commandment, but it's great advice. Now, King Solomon wasn't saying, "Goof off and play all day."

Kids played back then, but they also did chores. And he wasn't saying, "Enjoy yourself now, 'cause it's only work when you get older." It's in the attitude. Anybody at any age can enjoy life. Like Solomon said, "However many years anyone may live, let them enjoy them all" (verse 8).

Kids are hardwired to want to have fun, and as long as your homework and chores are done, go for it! We all need to unwind after a hard day. But it helps to have a positive attitude about school, homework, and chores too. If you complain about them, it'll seem like it takes forever to get through them. Hey, things really aren't so bad. You're not shoveling chicken dung all day long. Whatever the chore, plant the thought in your mind, *"I have to do this so I might as well have a good attitude."* Even if you don't enjoy it, you can whistle while you work. Well, not out loud during a math test, but in other words, have a positive attitude. It beats whining while you work.

Put your heart into your work and try to enjoy it. It'll make things go faster. Then you'll be done sooner and can have some real fun.

Make a list of the things you enjoy doing. How can you make sure you budget time to have fun?

DAY 50

PART OF THE PRIDE

Pursue righteousness, faith, love and peace, along with those who call on the Lord out of a pure heart.

2 TIMOTHY 2:22

To pursue means "to chase or to follow." You know, like a lion pursues a zebra across the savannah. (Run, zebra! Run!) So the Bible tells you to set your sights on good stuff like righteousness, faith, love, and peace—and then to chase those things nonstop. And don't just go after these things alone. Just like lions hunt in teams, it works best when you pursue good stuff with other Christians. (Scratch one zebra.)

There's an old saying: "If you run with wolves, you'll learn to howl like a wolf." Well, if you run with weasels, you'll start squeaking like a weasel. The point is that if you spend time with a bad crowd, they influence you, right? Hang with a smoking, cursing crowd, and the odds are you'll end up smoking and swearing. (At least you'll be breathing secondhand smoke and getting an earful of curses.) Or if your friends watch trashy movies, they'll try to suck you into that too.

It's great to have cool friends who do exciting stuff, but remember: You can do cool, fun stuff with Christians. Believers can have lots of fun too! It's okay to have non-Christian friends, but your closest pals should be other Christians—you know, guys "who call on the Lord." The fun stuff you do can include praying with them and studying the Bible together. Instead of getting into all the wrong stuff, these dudes are doing what's right. So run with lions—not with weasels.

Name some advantages of having Christian friends.

DAY 51

HE WHO WORSHIPS GOD, WINS!

Jesus said to him, "Away from me, Satan! For it is written, 'Worship the Lord your God, and serve him only.'

MATTHEW 4:10

One day the devil tried to tempt Jesus. He showed Jesus all the kingdoms of this world and their glittering splendor and fabulous riches. The devil said, "All this I will give you . . . if you will bow down and worship me" (Matthew 4:9). Jesus told Satan to get away, and then he quoted Scripture, saying that we are to worship God instead—and only God.

The devil doesn't usually come out so bold. Usually he's happy if he can just get you to worship your belongings and your toys—anything but God. See, Jesus said that the first and greatest commandment was to love God with all your heart, but a lot of people think the number one rule is to get as many toys as they can just to enjoy life. Their motto is, "He who has the most toys when he dies, wins." Wrong!

The Bible says that greed is just like idol worship (Colossians 3:5). Now, there's nothing wrong with having toys or fancy new gadgets. It's okay to like them and think they're cool and take good care of them. But the problem is if you obsess over your stuff or put material things before God. Then it becomes like idol worship—like you are worshipping a thing instead of God.

Enjoy the toys and things that God has given you. Just remember that God is the one who gives you cool stuff to enjoy—so make God number one in your life.

What is the difference between idolizing something and simply enjoying it?

DAY 52

JESUS' RETURN FROM HEAVEN

People will see the Son of Man coming in clouds with great power and glory. And he will send his angels and gather his elect from the four winds.

MARK 13:26–27

Christians have different ideas about what earth's final days will be like. The book of Revelation is deep and mysterious, so we don't understand it all—yet. But one thing Jesus was very clear about is that he will return one day. When he comes back in the sky, people all around the planet will see him. For two thousand years, Christians have waited for Jesus to return and end all wars and famines and set up the perfect kingdom of God on earth. Christians living today want the same thing. Or maybe you hope Jesus will wait awhile. Maybe you want to grow up, graduate high school, and do stuff first. Maybe you don't want this world to end quite yet.

Don't worry. Jesus' kingdom will be a whole lot more fun than life right now. It's not like we're going to leave earth and then float around on clouds forever. Some Christians think that after taking us to heaven for a wonderful time with him and all the Christians who have ever lived, we'll return to earth. Then, instead of selfish, greedy people running the place, there will be love, peace, and harmony on earth.

We don't know all the details of Jesus' return. But we do know that he is coming back one day with power and great glory, and that life will be better than it's ever been.

What do you most look forward to in Jesus' coming kingdom?

DAY 53

NOT COOL!

A drunkard staggers around in his vomit.

ISAIAH 19:14

In Bible times, beer and wine were plentiful. Like today, some people had no control over their drinking once they started. The first cupful was followed by a second and a third until they got so drunk they were down on all fours barking like a dog. Some were even staggering around and vomiting on themselves and anyone else who happened to be near them.

Sometimes you hear teens say, "You shoulda seen Billy at the party. He was so drunk he was puking over the rail. Then he fell off the back porch and rolled around in his vomit."

Everyone laughs, and Billy stands there grinning. He imagines the other kids are thinking, *Wow! How cool! What a man!* Hello? Wallowing around in your own foul-smelling whitewash is cool? Some people's definition of a fun time is pretty weird.

Whatever your parents think about alcohol, or whatever your church's doctrine is on wine, you must definitely not touch it. It's against the law for kids to drink alcohol. So what if some so-called friends mock you for saying no. You have nothing to prove to them. In fact, if they pressure you to drink, ditch them. You go your way and let them go their way. There's nothing grown-up or macho about kids drinking and staggering around in their half-digested dinner barf. So avoid that whole scene.

It's wise to be prepared in advance. How will you respond if someone offers you alcohol?

DAY 54

FOLLOW THROUGH

"Son, go and work today in the vineyard . . ." He answered, "I will, sir," but he did not go.

MATTHEW 21:28, 30

Jesus told a story about a farmer who had two sons. The farmer said to Son One, "Son, go and work today in the vineyard." Son One grunted no, so Dad told Son Two to take care of the vines. This guy promised, "I will, sir." But he never went. Well, that was some help! Fortunately, Son One felt so bad about telling his dad no that he went and worked.

Lots of kids are like the second son. They promise, "Sure, I'll do it," but only because saying no would cause trouble. Either that, or they say yes, go right on playing, and forget to follow through. So by bedtime the garbage still isn't out on the curb, the LEGO bricks are still covering the bedroom floor three inches deep, and the dog's so hungry it eats the hamster. And then the son hears his name being called . . .

Here's how to avoid that scene: When your parents tell

you to do something, give them your full attention and listen to what they're saying so you know you got it. Then—unless it's simply impossible—do the chore immediately. That way, the garbage gets put out, the LEGO bricks get picked up, the dog gets fed, and the hamster lives.

You need to follow through on your promises. Be a man of your word. If you promise you'll do something, do it.

Why is it important to always follow through and keep your promises?

DAY 55

REMEMBERING TO SAY THANKS

One of them, when he saw he was healed, came back, praising God in a loud voice. He threw himself at Jesus' feet and thanked him—and he was a Samaritan.

LUKE 17:15-16

Leprosy is a serious skin disease. Back in Bible days, leprosy ate away at a person's flesh until it finally killed him. What's more, it was very contagious. In Jesus' day there was no known cure for it. You think anyone wanted to hang around with the lepers? One time Jesus miraculously healed ten lepers, and nine of them ran off happy and never came back. Only one returned to say thanks—and he was so happy that he threw himself down at Jesus' feet in gratitude. And catch those last words: ". . . he was a Samaritan."

First notice what a big deal Jesus' actions were. He didn't avoid the lepers like everyone else did. He talked to them. And most importantly, he healed them. Ah, but only one came back to say "thank you." And he was a Samaritan, one of those with whom Jews did not get along well. In Jesus' day, Jews thought so little of Samaritans that when they'd see one coming the other direction they'd cross the street just so they wouldn't have to walk next to him.

Yet Scripture points out that of all those who were healed of this life-threatening illness, only the one the Jews liked the least was considerate enough to thank Christ for the gift.

This is still a great message for us today—God does not care one little bit about a person's race or from where he comes. His love is available freely to everyone. And in the same way we ought to love all people without regard to their background or race.

Make a list of a few things you are thankful for. Do you make it a regular habit to thank God for all the ways he blesses you?

DAY 56

HAPPY THOUGHTS VS. SICKNESS

A cheerful heart is good medicine, but a crushed spirit dries up the bones.

PROVERBS 17:22

They didn't have a lot of medicines back in the days when Solomon wrote this, and they certainly had no X-rays or antibiotics. But Solomon realized a very important fact: "a crushed spirit dries up the bones." Not literally, of course. You won't turn into a fossil. But when you're seriously discouraged, it's like you have the energy drained right out of you. You don't feel like doing anything.

The thoughts that you think can affect your health. If you constantly worry, or you're bummed out day after day, or you have a negative, angry attitude, it can actually make you ill. You don't need to have some bozo sneeze in your face to get sick. You can make yourself sick simply by thinking downer thoughts all the time. These are called psychosomatic (sy-ko-so-mat-ik) illnesses.

On the other hand, having a cheerful heart is like good medicine. Science has proved this. Hospital patients have sometimes improved their health by watching slapstick comedy shows and laughing their heads off. God designed it so that when you laugh, your brain releases healing chemicals into your bloodstream. And hey, trusting God and being happy because God loves you works wonders! Nehemiah 8:10 says, "The joy of the LORD is your strength."

Want to stay healthy and strong? The next time you're tempted to drag yourself around in a grumpy, growling mood, stay focused on positive, happy thoughts instead!

What types of things make you laugh and improve your mood?

DAY 57

PLUNGING INTO THE SEWERS

They are surprised that you do not join them in their reckless, wild living, and they heap abuse on you.

1 PETER 4:4

Back in New Testament days, many Greeks and Romans enjoyed wild, drunken parties and sexual immorality. Unwise people went whole hog into wild pleasure with no sense of right and wrong. Well, these guys were plunging into a flood of hog-wild pleasure, whooping and laughing as they did. They thought it was great, and if some Christian didn't agree, they'd dump verbal abuse on him.

Some kids today have that attitude. They'll steal and laugh about it, vandalize someone's property and think it's cool, or watch X-rated movies and visit pornographic Internet sites and think that's perfectly normal. To them, someone who's not into that trash is strange. Their problem, right? But what if they pressure us to join them?

If our town flooded and the sewer lines were backed up into Main Street, and some kids were swimming in it, would we dive in with them? No. Well, we shouldn't jump into this flood either. Sure, we may get called a "mama's boy" if we refuse to join them. They may swear at us and call us all kinds of names, but remember: They are the ones who are truly strange.

Do what's right even if some kids mock you for it. It's no fun being called names, but it sure beats plunging into the toilet just to belong.

How do you deal with peer pressure? What are some wise ways to respond when other kids pressure you?

DAY 58

BRING HONOR TO YOUR PARENTS

A wise son brings joy to his father, but a foolish son brings grief to his mother.

PROVERBS 10:1

You don't have to be an Einstein to be wise. When the Bible talks about being wise, it's not talking about being clever or being such a brain that you get 100 percent on every test. Sure, that'll make your parents happy, but wise means a deeper kind of intelligence—it means perceiving God's ways and following them. That will bring your folks real joy.

Now, you can't live your life concerned about people's opinions, but it is important to be concerned about your parents' opinions. You need to be careful that what you do brings them joy and honor instead of grief and disgrace. The Bible says, "Honor your father and mother," so you have to think about how your actions will bring honor to them. How can you do that?

To honor your parents, you must respect their authority and obey them. But if they're not around when you have to make a choice—to go along with something or not to—you honor your parents by doing the right thing and making godly choices. Hey, we all slip up and make bad choices sometimes. But the question is: What kind of choices are you in the habit of making day after day?

If you continually misbehave, you bring dishonor on yourself and on your parents. When you continually behave wisely, you bring honor and joy to yourself and to your parents.

Why is it important to do the right thing even when your parents or other authority figures aren't looking?

IF YOU CONTINUALLY MISBEHAVE, YOU BRING DISHONOR ON YOURSELF AND ON YOUR PARENTS. WHEN YOU CONTINUALLY BEHAVE WISELY, YOU BRING HONOR AND JOY TO YOURSELF AND TO YOUR PARENTS.

DAY 59

HARD WORK IS WORTH IT

When he sees . . . how pleasant is his land, he will bend his shoulder to the burden.

GENESIS 49:14–15

Thousands of years ago a guy named Jacob had twelve sons. When Jacob blessed his sons, he compared his son Issachar (Issa-car) to a donkey. A donkey is a strong beast that—if it is motivated—can work hard and carry heavy saddlebags. Issachar liked to lie around resting as much as the next guy, but when he caught the vision of how good life could be if he worked, he put out.

It's the same today. A part-time job mowing yards is hard work. You can't sit at home watching TV if it's time to mow lawns. So what motivates you to get off the couch, strap on your skates, and pull your cart full of papers down the street? Money, and the good stuff it can buy, makes it worth it.

Hard work is just that—hard work—but it's worth it. Maybe your parents and grandparents give you stuff now, but the older you get the more you have to start earning your own way. And in the world out there, you don't get something for nothing. Maybe you'd rather spend time playing Xbox or PlayStation rather than mow the lawn, but unless you find a way to raise cash, you won't be able to buy the new game when you've defeated every level in the old one.

Do you need cash to buy some cool stuff? Then find some paying jobs and "bend your shoulder to the burden."

What kind of odd jobs do you enjoy doing? Could you turn that into a way to earn spending money?

DAY 60

TEMPTATION

Flee the evil desires of youth.

2 TIMOTHY 2:22

When the apostle Paul was in prison for being a Christian, he wrote a letter to a young friend named Timothy. Paul warned, "Flee the evil desires of youth." Now, why did he say that? Because a Christian named Demas had just been derailed by evil desires. Paul said, "Demas, because he loved this world, has deserted me" (2 Timothy 4:10).

We don't know what exactly Demas was tempted by, but it totally stopped him from following Jesus. Paul didn't want Timothy to go down too. Things like skateboarding, mountain biking, soccer, and swimming are good. There's nothing evil about desiring to do these things. And movies and video games can be cool. But there are evil movies and video games that you shouldn't desire. And even perfectly normal desires—like a man's desire for sex—can become evil desires if you're not supposed to have them yet.

When it comes to the good stuff you love doing, enjoy it. But wait for things you're supposed to wait for and stay away from evil stuff you're supposed to stay away from. You know what kinds of things tempt you, so be on guard. Your parents know too, so if they warn you that you're getting too close, listen to them. Paul watched out for Timothy; your parents watch out for you.

Don't stand there staring at the temptation while you're trying to resist it. Walk away. In fact, if the temptation is strong, flee!

List a few areas you struggle with temptation. What are some practical ways you can resist temptation?

DAY 61

CHOOSING CHRISTLIKE COACHES

Follow my example, as I follow the example of Christ.

1 CORINTHIANS 11:1

The apostle Paul had been chatting about his personal lifestyle. He had explained how he wasn't seeking his own good, but trying to live unselfishly to help others. Jesus had said to love God and love others and live as a Christian, and though Paul wasn't perfect, he was doing his best to do those things. That's why he could tell others to follow his example.

When you're trying to learn something, it's important to listen to someone who knows what he's talking about and is living what he preaches. If you want to learn to play football better, you listen to your coach, not some kindergartener who doesn't know the first thing about the game, right? So if you want to learn to follow Christ, whose example do you follow—some Hollywood actor whose life is one big train wreck?

If you're trying to follow Jesus, you need to follow role models who are genuinely trying to obey God. Paul was like a coach to the early Christians—and we all need coaches and instructors. Sure, you know you're supposed to love your neighbor, but there's more to Christianity than that. Just like there's more to football than just "grab the ball and run." And who's gonna teach you this stuff? The guys who know it inside out.

Just like you constantly need to improve your game, you need to learn more about the Christian life and walking with God. Choose life-coaches who follow Jesus.

Who are your role models in the Christian faith? How can you learn from them?

DAY 62

WARS ON THE EVENING NEWS

You will hear of wars and rumors of wars, but see to it that you are not alarmed. Such things must happen, but the end is still to come.

MATTHEW 24:6

Jesus' disciples had just finished asking, "What will be the sign of your coming, and of the end of the age?" Jesus told them what to look for, but part of his answer was telling them what not to get worried about. "You'll hear about wars. Don't get alarmed. You'll hear that a war might start. Don't freak out. Wars are bad, but they're not necessarily the end of the world."

These days, with newsmen reporting right from war zones and blown-up cars smoking all over your TV screen, it may feel like the war is happening in your living room. You've heard that one day the Battle of Armageddon will mean the end of the world, so maybe you get worried that some new battle you see on TV is going to start it. Or maybe you see some guy carrying signs that read: "Armageddon has begun!"

It's natural to worry, but don't. Don't lose sleep over it. Jesus specifically said not to be alarmed. He wants us to be comforted by the knowledge that no matter what happens, God is in control and we are in his hands. Wars have been happening since the beginning of civilization. Jesus told us that these things must happen. War is serious business, and lots of people suffer in wars. So pray for the people involved.

Jesus knows that people often worry when serious stuff is happening, and that's why he warned us not to worry or get alarmed.

Write down the things you worry about. The next time you begin to worry make it a point to pray instead.

DAY 63

HANGING WITH UNCOOL KIDS

Do not be proud, but be willing to associate with people of low position. Do not be conceited.

ROMANS 12:16

In the days of the early church, some Christians came from rich and powerful families, while many were poor or even slaves. When the church met to worship God, all different classes came together. Christians were taught to treat rich and poor the same in church. Some rich Christians were willing to do that, but no way they wanted to be seen with workers and slaves throughout the week.

The same thing happens today. Some kids are okay with hanging out with certain kids in church or at family gatherings, but when they get around cool kids they don't want to associate with un-cool kids anymore. Paul said people who do that are conceited and proud. They have a high opinion of themselves and think they're too good for others.

You may know some other kid who really needs to hear this, but for now, apply it to your life. Do you sometimes let other kids or your own pride tell you who you can be seen with or can't be seen with? In God's eyes, being rich or poor, having a cool rep or being nobody special means nothing. And think about it: Most kids believe that everyone is created equal. They know when someone's acting uppity.

Don't be proud or conceited. Hang out with Christians who are different or poorer or richer or cooler or less cool than you.

Is there someone you know who needs a friend? How can you reach out?

DAY 64

WHEN DONKEYS FALL DOWN

If you see the donkey of someone who hates you fallen down under its load, do not leave it there; be sure you help them with it.

EXODUS 23:5

The Ten Commandments told the Israelites not to steal from their fellow man, not to lie about him or hurt him or long for his belongings. Some Israelites did all that, but if they saw one of their enemies struggling to get a fallen donkey back on its feet—they'd walk past, snickering, "I'm not hurting ol' Jethro here, but I'm sure not helping him." God said no deal. Even if the guy hates you, help him.

Okay, so most kids who hate you don't own donkeys, so does this verse not apply? Does that mean that if a kid who always bothers you is riding home from school and he spills his backpack on the ground, that you can just walk by laughing and say, "That's his problem"? After all, a backpack isn't a donkey, right?

No, and his bike isn't a donkey either, but it's the principle of the thing. God wants you to help people who need help, not just walk past. So if you see a "nerd" drop his books in school, stop and help him. If some enemy tumbles on his bicycle, help him up. It's called being considerate. Besides, it might turn an enemy into a friend.

Can you remember a time when someone helped you? How did their kindness make you feel?

DAY 65

FAVORITE FRIENDS AND FAVORITISM

If you really keep the royal law found in Scripture, "Love your neighbor as yourself," you are doing right. But if you show favoritism, you sin.

JAMES 2:8-9

"Love your neighbor as yourself" is the foundation for almost half of the Ten Commandments. Love your neighbor as you love yourself and you won't steal from him, hurt him, or lie about him. But the catch is, you should do good to all people, not just close friends, not just those who can do you favors in return. If you treat a friend extra-good but treat another kid like dirt, you're breaking the Royal Law.

We all tend to do stuff for our friends that we wouldn't do for others. Jesus zeroed in on this when he pointed out that even tax collectors were kind to their buddies. Even people who cared less about God had enough manners to greet their pals when they saw them (Matthew 5:46–47). Doing this had nothing to do with having the love of Christ in their lives.

If we care about everyone, not just our buddies, then we'll start treating all people the way God wants us to. Sure, we may hang out with certain guys 'cause we're interested in the same things. It's okay to have close friends we spend most of our time with. It's cool to do things for our buddies. But let's not get a clique mentality and ignore everyone else.

Want to do the right thing? Keep God's Royal Law—love others as much as you love yourself. And don't just love some of them. Love them all.

List a few ways you can show kindness to those around you.

DAY 66

WISDOM VERSUS BOOK LEARNING

How did this man get such learning without having been taught?

JOHN 7:15

Jewish boys went to school in Jesus' day, but their education was mostly memorizing the laws of Moses, discussing the laws' details, and learning to read and write. And that was it.

If a young guy wanted more education, he had to find a teacher (rabbi) and study under him. Jesus didn't do that. When he finished school, he went to work full-time as a carpenter. So where did he get his massive wisdom and learning? From God, his Father!

Unless your family's plane crashed on a tropical island and all you learned while growing up was how to wrestle sharks and climb coconut palms, chances are you'll get a decent education. But you'd be surprised at how many high school graduates don't know important stuff like how to use a credit card wisely, how to take care of a car, how to do their laundry, and how to relate to others. Some are especially clueless when it comes to spiritual stuff.

You can learn about credit cards, cars, and laundry simply by living life. But when it comes to the important spiritual stuff, you need to really love God, spend time with him, and learn from him. You can go to Bible school—that'll help a lot—but it's more important to read your Bible yourself and have a relationship with God.

God can give you wisdom, so pray and ask him to start giving you the kind of deep wisdom you can't learn from just reading textbooks.

In what areas would you like to grow in wisdom?

DAY 67

THINGS IN COMMON

Do not be yoked together with unbelievers. For what do righteousness and wickedness have in common?

2 CORINTHIANS 6:14

Not being "yoked together with unbelievers" doesn't mean standing back while atheists are egged. Rather, it comes from Moses' law to not put a wooden yoke on the neck of an ox and a mule at the same time, to make them pull a plow together (Deuteronomy 22:10). It just doesn't work well. It's like you trying to run a three-legged race tied to a toddler. In the same way, Christians shouldn't be "yoked together" with unbelievers.

Okay, it's a no-brainer that if kids are into wicked weirdness and joking about dark, sick stuff, you should avoid them. Don't be pals with them. But does this mean that you shouldn't have any non-Christian friends? Does it mean that you should only play baseball with kids from your church or you can't talk to kids of another religion?

No, thank goodness, it doesn't mean that. You can and

should be friendly toward all people, no matter how they look, what religion they are, or whether they believe in God or not. But being friendly doesn't mean you super-glue your jackets together. Being "yoked together" is a close relationship, and your closest friends should be fellow Christians. That way when you are in times of need, the advice you get from your closest friends lines up with Christ's teaching.

You may have to play on the same baseball team as a wicked kid, but you need a whole lot more than baseball in common before you make him a close friend.

Make a list of your closest friends. Why is it important for your closest friends to be fellow Christians?

DAY 68

JOINING A GANG—OR NOT

My son, if sinful men entice you, do not give in to them . . . do not go along with them, do not set foot on their paths.

PROVERBS 1:10, 15

King Solomon talked about a gang who killed and robbed the innocent. They were recruiting new gang members and tempted youth by promising them easy money if they joined. All they had to do was murder and rob travelers and they'd be rich. Solomon warned that no matter how much criminals entice you, don't set foot on their evil path.

You don't have to join a criminal organization to be part of a "gang." It could simply be a group of tough kids pressuring you to join them. To prove you're with them, you have to steal something, hurt somebody, or vandalize some property. Or some drug pusher might offer you easy money if you start peddling drugs and get other kids hooked on drugs.

If kids tempt you to do evil, don't give in. Don't even set foot on their paths. Don't even do one thing they say. That'll just give them something to use against you: "You've already done this, so what's so bad about doing this other thing?" Some kids really know how to work you over and put on the pressure, so don't even listen to them.

Sometimes "belonging" isn't worth it. No matter how cool gang membership seems at first, there's a very expensive price to pay, so keep your feet off their destructive path.

Write down a couple of ways you can resist peer pressure.

DAY 69

LIBRARIES AND LEARNING

A Jew named Apollos, a native of Alexandria . . . was a learned man, with a thorough knowledge of the Scriptures.

ACTS 18:24

Back in Roman times, the city of Alexandria, in Egypt, had the largest library on this planet. Like, half a million scrolls and books! It was a major center for learning. Some of the deepest thinkers went there to study and learn—and maybe to get lost in the dusty back aisles a few times. Apollos was one of those learned men. He not only learned math and science and history, but he also knew the Bible back to front and inside out. Some boys today devour books—especially comic books and manga—but they know practically nothing about the Bible. That's because they read those other books (sometimes over and over again), but when it comes to the Scriptures, they depend on adults to tell them the stories. Or they just get a bit of the action by reading Bible storybooks with big, bright pictures.

How did Apollos get his huge download of knowledge? He read every word in all those books. If you want to learn, you need to read. And while you're reading away, read your Bible, not just comics or storybooks. If you want the really good stuff, you've got to dive into the Good Book itself.

Having someone feed you spiritual food is okay when you're little, but when you get older, you've got to crack open the Bible and feed yourself.

What types of books do you enjoy reading? Why is it important to make reading the Bible a priority?

DAY 70

LOOKS JUST LIKE HIS DAD

Anyone who has seen me has seen the Father. How can you say, "Show us the Father"?

JOHN 14:9

Jesus' disciples knew that he was God's Son, but they wanted Jesus to show them his Father. They wanted to see God. Um . . . guys, listen, that's a bit of a problem. God the Father is invisible. You can't see him. But fortunately, Jesus is the "image of the invisible God" (Colossians 1:15). That's why, when God decided to give people a clear idea of what he was like, he sent his son, Jesus, to live on earth as a man.

Maybe you wish you could see God. Actually, even if you could, it's not such a great idea. There's a reason God made himself invisible. God's so powerful that if you look directly at his face, you'll fall over dead. God told Moses, "You cannot see my face, for no one may see me and live" (Exodus 33:20). It'd be like lying down on a launching pad under a rocket so you can get a good, close look at its engines firing up. It's just not a good idea.

You're best looking at Jesus. But you say, "How can I? He's not on earth anymore." Listen, knowing what Jesus is like does not mean seeing how big his nose is, what color his hair is, or if his eyes get crinkle lines when he smiles. That's not the important stuff. In fact, the Gospels don't even describe how he looks. What's truly important is who Jesus was and how he lived!

If you want to see God, look at Jesus. And if you want to get a good look at Jesus, read all about his amazing life in the Gospels.

Make a list of things you know about Jesus' character. What was he like? What stands out to you?

DAY 71

DOING WHAT YOU CAN

If anyone has material possessions and sees a brother or sister in need but has no pity on them, how can the love of God be in that person?

1 JOHN 3:17

If you're a Christian and you see a person who really needs help, you'll have pity on him or her. And if you can help, God's love will move you to do something. Now, sometimes you can't help with money but you can pray for the person. But if you can help with physical resources and some kid's hungry or cold, it's no help at all to tell him that you hope he gets warm and fed and do nothing else. (See James 2:15–16.)

Of course, when you give you need to give wisely. If you've saved up your money and you're heading out to buy your mother a birthday present, you may see beggars asking for your money. While it is hard to tell if these people really need help, you can make sure you are giving to established organizations like your church or the Salvation Army, whose full-time jobs are helping those in need. Then when someone asks you for money, you can direct them to one of these places for help.

We can't solve all the world's problems, not even all the problems in our own towns, but often we can find places to help, even if they are only little things. These things can mean a lot. This can mean sharing our lunches with some kid who forgot his, giving away our old toys or clothes to charity, or suggesting that your family sponsor a child in a poor country. There's no end of things we can do.

Write down a few different ways you can be generous to your family and friends.

DAY 72

TURN THE OTHER CHEEK

cheek also.

MATTHEW 5:39

Jesus said that if someone strikes you on the cheek, don't start fighting. In fact, offer him your other cheek too. Now, some Christians think this means that if someone starts slugging you, you're supposed to let him keep punching your teeth in. Even if he's beating you to a pulp, you're not supposed to defend yourself. Wrong! In today's passage, Jesus used the Greek word *rhapizein*, which means to slap. You don't usually get hurt from a slap. It's more of an insult than anything.

If you're hotheaded and someone insults you, you probably start screaming insults back. If you lose your temper easily, other kids may have fun provoking you into shouting matches and fights. Don't let them. That bozo with a big mouth isn't taking anything away from you. Don't let him egg you into fights.

If someone's insulting you, it's a reflection of his bad attitude. He may act that way because he has low self-esteem and is trying to feel better about himself at your expense. Letting it pass is a sign of strength. But if someone actually starts slugging you, don't hesitate to defend yourself by telling an adult. Assault (attacking someone) is a crime; it's against the law.

Be patient toward immature kids and show them God's love. That is called "turning the other cheek." But make sure they understand that they can't just walk all over you.

It takes wisdom to know when to overlook an offense and when to tell an adult. What are some things to consider when you make those decisions?

DAY 73

FLAT FLATTERY

Such people are not serving our Lord Christ . . . By smooth talk and flattery they deceive the minds of naive people.

ROMANS 16:18

Paul warned Christians in Rome to watch out for those who came teaching a different message than he'd taught them. These Christians had heard the truth, but now false teachers were moving in and dumping weird stuff on them. These false teachers knew how to deceive the naive (people who are not very wise about the world). How? They used flattery and said stuff like, "Oh, you're so special! That's why I'm telling you this secret, special stuff."

There are smooth-talking deceivers around today too. If someone said to you, "The Bible doesn't say such-and-such is wrong," you might say, "Cool! I've always wanted to do that!" Another false teacher may be in the form of popular books and movies. If some author writes a book telling outrageous lies about Jesus—that he was a magician or that he never died on the cross—the book becomes a bestseller.

The best way to avoid being tricked by smooth talkers is to read your Bible. Know what it says and doesn't say. That way you won't believe every fast-talking trickster who makes a false claim. Of course, sometimes you won't know where in the Bible to find an answer, so ask your parents or your pastor. They've usually spent years studying it. They'll know.

If some smooth talker tries scrambling your brain by telling you weird stuff about the Bible, tell him you're not in the baloney-buying business. Then avoid him.

List a few reasons why it's important to know your Bible.

DAY 74

A "TOUGH TIMES" BROTHER

A friend loves at all times, and a brother is born for a time of adversity.

PROVERBS 17:17

A true friend loves at all times, meaning he doesn't give up on his friends when something happens and they're not much fun to be around anymore. He sticks with his friends. And when our brothers are going through adversity (tough times), they should be able to count on us to be there for him. We were literally born for that purpose.

It can be hard on us when someone in our family is going through adversity. Maybe one of them ends up sick for a long time and can't run around and do back flips on the trampoline anymore. Or maybe that person's friends have dumped him or her and now that person wants to hang out with us more than we care for. Or maybe he or she is grounded because the latest report card was not so acceptable. We can be there for those friends, but it'll mean missing other fun stuff.

Being a friend isn't all fun and games; sometimes it means sacrificing what we want to do. But being a friend has always been about more than just playing with someone. Being a friend means you don't pull some amazing vanishing act when your friend is in trouble or gets sick. A friend loves at all times—not just sometimes and not just during fun times.

Be a true brother to your brothers and, yes, to your sisters as well. You'd want them to be there for you if you were going through rough times, right?

Can you think of a time when a friend stuck by you during a tough time? How can you be that type of friend to others?

DAY 75

TURNING ON THE TAP

For the mouth speaks what the heart is full of. A good man brings good things out of the good stored up in him, and an evil man brings evil things out of the evil stored up in him.

MATTHEW 12:34-35

You constantly take in sights and sounds and fill your mind with images. So when your tongue starts wagging, it draws on what's stored in your brain. If 80 percent of your brain cells are taken up by soccer knowledge, chances are high you'll talk about soccer. Sure, you can try to talk only about the knowledge that fills the other 20 percent, but when you're full of a subject, it eventually flows out of your mouth.

Let's say you spend a lot of time playing violent video games and watching TV shows and movies where kids have bad attitudes and bad mouths. Do you really think that stuff will have no effect on the way you think and talk? Some kids argue, "I just like that stuff. I wouldn't actually talk about it or do it." Not at first, maybe, but eventually when your mind is used to it, yes, you will.

The flip side of the coin is that if you focus on good stuff, then good stuff will fill your mind so much that it will overflow and come out your mouth. That doesn't mean you should talk only about Bible verses or watch only Christian videos. There's lots of good stuff out there. Have a good attitude about whatever you think or talk about—from sports to girls.

What you spend your time thinking about and reading and watching really does matter!

What are some good things (books, TV shows, entertainment) that are a positive influence?

DAY 76

HEALTHY AND UNHEALTHY AMBITION

Do nothing out of selfish ambition or vain conceit. Rather, in humility value others above yourselves, not looking to your own interests but each of you to the interests of the others.

PHILIPPIANS 2:3-4

There's nothing wrong with ambition. But there's a huge problem with selfish ambition. That's when people have a "me-first" attitude, are only looking out for their own interests and could care less about the other guy. People get like that when they're conceited—worse yet, vainly conceited—and figure they're better than others and deserve more.

Okay, so if you're looking out for the other guy's interests, not just your own, does that mean that you shouldn't be competitive? Should you let him win a video game? (Not likely.)

Does it mean you shouldn't do your best in a spelling bee? (No.) Or does it mean that you can be competitive, just don't gloat as the other person loses? (You're getting warm.)

God wants you to really work at things and to do your best, in relationships, in sports, in schoolwork or business. But in doing your best you also need to love others—look out for what's best for them, not just what's best for you. To live this way is to live with the mind of Christ. It is living your life as he lived his life.

The cure for being vainly conceited or having selfish ambition is to care for others. If you're looking out for others too, you'll think of their needs and feelings as well.

How would you describe the difference between ambition and selfish ambition?

DAY 77

YOUR PERSONAL TRAINER

Train yourself to be godly. For physical training is of some value, but godliness has value for all things.

1 TIMOTHY 4:7–8

Physical training is of some value, all right! Exercise and self-discipline do good stuff for your body, making you stronger, faster, and better at sports. Whether you have a personal trainer advising you how to zing the badminton birdie low over the net, a guy beside the pool showing you how to swim faster than a piranha, or a martial arts instructor teaching you how to block a punch, it's all good.

When you train, you improve your technique—slide into home base sneakier, slice through the water faster, or kick through a brick wall harder (just kidding). You learn about mistakes you've been making and how to improve—pacing yourself to not wear out quickly and cutting down your time.

The apostle Paul compared sports training to living a Christian life. It takes the same self-discipline and the same focus on the goal—only the results are better than a trophy. If you always try to do the right thing, you become a better person all around. By the way, you have to "train yourself to be godly," but you don't have to do it alone. God is your trainer and he's always with you.

Just as physical training is good for your physical health, spiritual training is good for your spiritual health and your whole life! Do your best—both in sports and in your walk with God.

What sports do you enjoy? What similarities does sports training have with the Christian life?

JUST AS PHYSICAL TRAINING IS GOOD FOR YOUR PHYSICAL HEALTH, SPIRITUAL TRAINING IS GOOD FOR YOUR SPIRITUAL HEALTH AND YOUR WHOLE LIFE!

DAY 78

LUST OF THE EYES

Everything in the world—the lust of the flesh, the lust of the eyes . . . comes not from the Father but from the world.

1 JOHN 2:16

Tons of TV ads show pretty women selling something while dressed in almost nothing. What's the big idea? Can't they afford clothes? Oh, yeah, they can. Those bikinis are their work clothes. See, automobile companies and other advertisers want to get men's attention, and since they know that guys are interested in sex, the advertisers bring on the beach babes.

This is why there are "men's" sites online and "adult" channels on TV. All these X-rated images that feed the "cravings of sinful man" and the "lust of the eyes" are called pornography. (*Pornography* comes from the Greek word *porne*, which means "to sell sex for cash.") Now, it's fine to notice that a girl is beautiful, but the problem with staring at porn is that it gets your mind working overtime, craving sex—and that leads to trouble.

God loves human beings. To make sure humans keep

having children, God programmed men to be very attracted to women, and he made sex very enjoyable. But here's the deal: God wants you to enjoy sex within marriage—not before marriage, not outside of marriage. To be sure you got that point, he spelled out some rules in the Bible. Obey them and you'll steer clear of problems. Make up your mind that you'll honor God by keeping your eyes away from pornography.

What are some practical ways you can avoid pornography online and on TV?

DAY 79

ABSOLUTE PURITY

Treat . . . younger women as sisters, with absolute purity.

1 TIMOTHY 5:1–2

Paul's advice to young men was straightforward: Respect everyone. Respect older men as if they were your dad and older women as if they were your mom. Treat the guys in your church as if they were your brothers and the girls as if they were your sisters. Of course, all these people don't live in your house with you, but they are part of your spiritual family. And this verse focuses on treating girls with respect.

Of course, Paul's advice won't make sense if you punch your sister or tease her. "Yeah," you say, "but my sister teases me. Am I supposed to be kind to her when she bugs me?" Well, if she does that, talk to your parents about it and let them deal with her. In the meantime be patient and kind to your sister. Then turn around and treat all girls the same way.

And don't forget the "with absolute purity" part. Girls are

special people created by God. They're not sexual objects to make dumb jokes about. Don't hang around with guys who make inappropriate comments about girls; otherwise, you'll end up spewing out their same brain garbage. Tell them to cut it out, and if they don't, then you cut out of there.

If you respect someone, you don't say bad things about him or her. You don't even think bad things about them. That's the attitude God wants you to have toward girls.

Why is it important to show respect to all people?

DAY 80

CHURCH—BELIEVERS BELONG TOGETHER

Let us . . . not give up meeting together, as some are in the habit of doing, but encourage one another.

HEBREWS 10:24–25

In the early church, believers were sometimes persecuted for being Christians. It could be dangerous to meet. All it took was one spy and you could all get arrested. But often things weren't so serious. A lot of people stopped attending meetings because they simply couldn't be bothered to go. They skipped so many services that they got in the habit of not going to church. Okay, if there's such a howling blizzard outside your door that the dog teams are freezing solid and even the penguins are falling over dead from frostbite, that's one thing. Or if your family is colonizing Mars, you can't zip back once a week to your hometown church. But hey, if your only reason for not going to church is because you want to sleep in or you just don't feel like going, that really doesn't cut it.

Sure, you can be a Christian all alone, but that's not God's plan. God made people to need other people—to belong to a community. It's important for Christians to go to church. It strengthens you when you spend time with other believers because you encourage each other. Worshiping with others inspires you. And your teachers have prepared important lessons from God's Word to teach you.

You won't always feel like going to church, but meeting with other Christians is a good habit to get into. So dig your dog team out of the snowdrifts, jump in the sled, and go.

Are you involved at church? If not, what can you do to get involved?

DAY 81

DEALING WITH PERSECUTION

Blessed are you when people hate you, when they exclude you and insult you . . . because of the Son of Man. Rejoice in that day and leap for joy, because great is your reward in heaven.

LUKE 6:22-23

Jesus knew that Christians would be persecuted for believing in him. There would be times when people would mock and insult them. Sometimes their former friends would snub them. So how are Christians supposed to deal with this kind of rejection? Jesus gave a surprising answer. He said that we were supposed to rejoice and be happy about it.

You're probably thinking that no way do you feel happy when kids tease you for believing in Jesus or for going to church. And you're not particularly glad when old pals don't hang around with you anymore because you stand up for what's right. Being cut from the herd can hurt. So how do you deal with it? And what about all this is supposed to make you happy?

First of all, you know you're being rejected or insulted because you're making God happy, and that ought to make you happy. And what should make you even happier is the knowledge that God has promised to bless you for standing up for Jesus. God is going to see to it that you receive a great reward in heaven for your troubles down here.

Leap for joy when other kids insult you? Hey, if you don't wanna leap, at least smile. Your future is very, very bright and blessed.

It's not out of the ordinary to be rejected or laughed at for being a Christian. How will you respond if that happens to you?

DAY 82

TAKING THE PLUNGE

Repent and be baptized . . . And you will receive the gift of the Holy Spirit.

ACTS 2:38

Believing in Jesus saves you, so why do you need to get baptized? Surely the water isn't washing away your sins. No. John the Baptist said to Jesus, "I baptize you with water, but he will baptize you with the Holy Spirit" (Mark 1:8). When you get saved, God's Holy Spirit enters your heart and cleanses you. Baptism is an outward symbol of what the Holy Spirit has done and a sign and seal of God's promises.

In the early church, Christians were baptized soon after they believed. Maybe you've believed in Jesus for years but you haven't taken the plunge yet. It's definitely something you should do. Now, different Christian churches have different views on when you should be baptized or exactly how you should be baptized, but the point is, if you're a believer, you should be baptized. The apostle Paul explained that baptism (going under the water) is kind of like dying and being buried. Then, "just as Christ was raised from the dead . . . we too may live a new life" (Romans 6:4). You then rise out of the water to new life. Got that? Just like Jesus died and came back to life, baptism is "death" to your old, selfish life. Bottom line: Baptism is a serious, public statement that you've made up your mind to live for Jesus.

Baptism is a huge step. It means turning from your selfish, self-centered ways and going all out for God. If you're a believer, baptism should be next on your list.

Have you been baptized? If not, talk to your parents and pastor about taking that step.

DAY 83

SAVE IT FOR MARRIAGE

It is God's will that you should . . . avoid sexual immorality.

1 THESSALONIANS 4:3

Two thousand years ago when boys grew into teens, their bodies went through huge changes. Their glands released a chemical called testosterone into their bodies that caused them to become very attracted to members of the opposite sex. And the news is testosterone is still doing its thing today. A gorgeous girl walks by and your heart slams around like a basketball, you sweat, and you may even become aroused. Often you can't help those reactions, but you *are* in control of what you do next.

As a Christian, you need to exercise self-control and save sex for marriage. Avoid sexual immorality. (That means stay away from breaking God's moral laws on sex.) Now, some teens say, "As long as you love a girl, it's okay to have sex with her." No, it's not. Besides, if she gets pregnant, the guy usually ditches her and lets her raise the baby alone. Hello? That's love? Moms and dads who protect and care for their kids—that's love.

"Cool" guys brag that they're having sex, but these same guys often get sexual diseases they're not bragging about. That includes penis warts and very painful sores called herpes. And then there's syphilis and AIDS. Sex outside of marriage is simply not God's will. Avoiding immorality is God's will.

God knows the problems that sexual immorality causes. That's why he said to avoid it. Just don't do it.

Why is God's way always best?

DAY 84

REWARD DAY FOR CHRISTIANS

We must all appear before the judgment seat of Christ, so that each of us may receive what is due us for the things done while in the body, whether good or bad.

2 CORINTHIANS 5:10

When you believe in Jesus, he gives you eternal life, and he prepares a fantastic place in heaven for you. But before you move into your home in paradise, you'll be required to show up at the judgment seat of Christ. Jesus will be your judge, and he'll examine everything you have ever done or said in your entire life.

Maybe you thought that after you left this world, you shot straight into heaven, ran up and down the streets of gold, moved into your new mansion, and maybe took off for a vacation to the moons of Jupiter. After all, all your sins have been forgiven, right? Right, they have. But before you do anything else, you'll have a serious, one-on-one appointment with Jesus Christ.

This is not to judge whether you go to heaven or not. If you love Jesus and have tried to do what he says, your destination's already settled. This session is to gloriously reward you for all the good you've ever done, and to burn away all the garbage you collected in your life. You'll be so happy about all the good you did, but crying about your selfish, bad deeds. Then Jesus will wipe all tears from your eyes.

Knowing that you'll appear before the judgment seat of Christ one day should remind you that what you do in this life really counts.

When it comes to "living a life that counts" what types of things should be on your list?

DAY 85

WHEN YOU JUDGE OTHERS

Do not judge, or you too will be judged. For in the same way you judge others, you will be judged.

MATTHEW 7:1–2

In Jesus' day, the Pharisees were trying too hard to be "righteous." Instead of looking at people's hearts and the good they were trying to do, they criticized people and passed judgment on them for every tiny rule they broke. Yet some Pharisees were guilty of more serious sins that they were jumping all over others about. But those who are not merciful will be judged without mercy themselves (James 2:13).

One problem with judging others (even just in your mind) is that sooner or later—usually sooner—your negative opinions come spilling out of your mouth and you start bad-mouthing that person. Also, often when you judge some kid as "bad" you usually start treating him badly too, because you figure a bad kid doesn't deserve to be treated well.

As Christians we realize that we have received mercy from God. Christ died for our sin instead of us having to pay for it. In the same way we must have mercy in judging others. Are they characterized by the wrong things they do? Or is this action an accident, or out of the ordinary for how they typically act? God desires that we be careful in how we evaluate others, choosing wisely between good and bad people and things.

If you must judge a situation—and sometimes you must—make sure that you judge others with love and kindness. Remember, God judges you the way you judge others.

Why is it wise to always show mercy and be kind to other people?

DAY 86

IMPRESSED HEARTS

These commandments that I give you today are to be on your hearts. Impress them on your children.

DEUTERONOMY 6:6-7

When God gave the Israelites the Ten Commandments (and all the other commands), he didn't just want his people to know about them. He wanted them to really, really know them. They had to have God's commands so deep in their hearts, they practically memorized them and obeyed them quickly and easily. Then they were supposed to impress them on their kids' hearts.

Speaking of impressing, ever take one of those plastic stamp thingies and press it on play dough? It leaves an impression. That's about how God wants his Word to be in your heart. If your parents or Sunday school teachers make you memorize Bible verses, they're helping get God's Word impressed in your heart. As David said, "I have hidden your word in my heart that I might not sin against you" (Psalm 119:11).

It may sometimes seem like a chore and a bore if your

mom and dad constantly teach you guidelines and laws, quote Bible verses to you, and write out lists of your duties. But that's what parents are supposed to do, because doing these things helps you in life. That was your most basic education before you even started going to school, and it'll continue to be a part of your learning curve as long as you're growing up.

When you really know God's commands and they're impressed deep on your heart, you're more likely to live by them. And that's the idea.

Have you ever memorized a Bible passage? Spend some time picking out a verse and commit it to memory.

DAY 87

GOD—ALWAYS MERCIFUL AND LOVING

Who is a God like you, who pardons sin and forgives the transgression. . . . You do not stay angry forever but delight to show mercy.

MICAH 7:18

Micah was a prophet of God, and he lived back when the tough Law of Moses was the law of the land. This was long before Jesus was born. Yet when Micah described God, he didn't talk about an angry God who loved to judge people when they goofed up. Micah said that God would rather forgive sin; he said God loved to show mercy.

Sometimes you might wonder, "Why was God mean and angry in the olden days, yet so loving and kind and forgiving after Jesus came?" Or maybe you've heard unbelievers ask,

"Why did God destroy cities and judge nations in the past, yet when Jesus came along he hugged little children and told us to love our enemies?" Why the change?

No change. God hasn't changed. God judged nations in the past because they rebelled against him, persecuted God's people, and did other bad things. And the news is: God still judges nations today. But God is not only into judgment and justice, he's also big on love. Even back in the olden days, he delighted in forgiveness.

God was forgiving and loving and merciful in the past, and he still is today. God said, "I the Lord do not change" (Malachi 3:6). God has always wanted to forgive.

How does it make you feel to know that God does not change? Does it bring you reassurance? Explain your thoughts.

DAY 88

TRUTH VERSUS MYTH

They will gather around them a great number of teachers to say what their itching ears want to hear. They will turn their ears away from the truth and turn aside to myths.

2 TIMOTHY 4:3-4

In Paul's day, some intellectual people liked the idea of a wise teacher named Jesus, but they freaked when Paul said that Jesus saved us by dying for our sins and then coming back to life. To them, that was too easy. They rejected the gospel and began inventing all kinds of complicated myths about Jesus.

Today, too, many people are "itchy" for something different. When their ears start itching like crazy, they figure the best way to scratch them is to stuff them full of interesting, bizarre theories. So they gather busloads of teachers and go gaga over old false books like the Gospel of Judas. (According to that so-called gospel, Judas was a hero for betraying Jesus!)

If you think those teachers with their myths are out to lunch, you've got that one right! The simple truth beats mixed-up myths any day. So how do you avoid swallowing interesting lies? By knowing what the Bible actually says about Jesus and by living for the truth. That way, when strange Bible teachers come along, your ears won't be itchy for their lies.

These days, lots of people turn their ears away from the truth because they don't want to hear it. Don't you do that. Read your Bible and listen to godly teachers.

What's the best way to spot lies?

THESE DAYS, LOTS OF PEOPLE TURN THEIR EARS AWAY FROM THE TRUTH BECAUSE THEY DON'T WANT TO HEAR IT. DON'T YOU DO THAT. READ YOUR BIBLE AND LISTEN TO GODLY TEACHERS.

DAY 89

WOMEN ON THE FRONT LINES

Greet Priscilla and Aquila, my co-workers in Christ Jesus. They risked their lives for me.

ROMANS 16:3–4

Priscilla and Aquila were Paul's pals, and this husband-wife team worked hard to help him preach the gospel. In fact, they did dangerous, secret-agent-type stuff and risked their lives to help him. Now, have you noticed that in the Old Testament the guys all have names, but often their wives' names aren't mentioned? Yet every time Priscilla and hubby Aquila are mentioned, she's not just named, but named first. Why? No one really knows why. All we know is that Priscilla was one famous, hardworking, gutsy gal.

If you read through the New Testament, you see how many outstanding women there were. Several women even traveled with Jesus and his disciples around Israel. And take a look around next time you're in church. Notice how many women and girls there are. And lots of women are pastors, Sunday school teachers, and missionaries. etc . . . Whoa! Women are on the front lines, doing a lot for God's kingdom!

God looks at people's hearts. He's interested in whether you love him and are willing to serve him. You're sitting in church enjoying the ride, but a whole lot of somebodies are working hard behind the scenes to keep things happening. A lot of those somebodies are women.

Women are very important to God. If you still have the idea that girls aren't as cool as guys, it's time to kick that thought out of your head.

▷ Name a few of the females you know who serve God and his kingdom.

DAY 90

WHEN FRIENDS DESERT YOU

You know that everyone in the province of Asia has deserted me, including Phygelus and Hermogenes.

2 TIMOTHY 1:15

The apostle Paul was arrested for being a leader of the Christians and soon he sat in a small, cold prison in Rome. That was bad enough. But what really hurt was when he learned that the Christians in the Roman province of Asia had turned against him. Paul had led these people to the Lord and he'd taught and trained them for years, but now they had turned against him. Talk about rejection!

It's hard when friends desert you—especially if you've been friends for a long time, you've done lots of fun stuff together, and you have good memories of them. Then suddenly they find "cooler" friends and ditch you. Or maybe someone starts a rumor about you, or tells a story about something dumb or embarrassing that you did, and suddenly your friends are gone.

It hurts when that happens. Paul doesn't get into detail about how he felt, but you know he was suffering. Jesus himself was rejected and told us that there'd be times when that would happen to us too. Times like that show you who your true friends are—the kind who stand by you no matter what—and God is your truest friend of all. He says, "Never will I leave you. Never will I forsake you" (Hebrews 13:5).

Paul had lost a lot of friends in Asia, but true friends like Timothy stayed close to him, and most important of all, God never abandoned him.

God will never abandon you. Why is that an important truth to remember?

DAY 91

LION ON THE LOOSE

Be alert and of sober mind. Your enemy the devil prowls around like a roaring lion looking for someone to devour. Resist him, standing firm in the faith.

1 PETER 5:8-9

The Bible warns, "Be alert!" In other words, watch out, because the devil is as fierce and as dangerous as a man-eating lion on the loose. He's looking for his next lunch. Don't let him ambush you. So what do you do when he attacks? Run? No. Even though he roars to scare you, stand firm. "Resist the devil, and he will flee from you" (James 4:7).

One of the devil's favorite tricks is to ambush you with temptation. But you can control yourself. It helps to decide ahead of time that you won't give in to temptation. Then you won't be caught off guard. Now, Jesus will protect you if you stay close to him. He will help you be strong so you can stand with your decisions.

Stand firm in your faith, resist temptation, resist the devil, and he will flee from you. And remember, it's not like you're so strong that you can resist the devil on your own. No, when you resist the devil's temptations, it is because he is fleeing from Jesus, who is inside you. It's Jesus who makes the devil afraid. Having Jesus close to you is like having a powerful security guard watching out for you. The devil may still be growling as he flees, but he will flee.

Keep on guard for the devil's attacks. If he does attack, stand firm and resist him. You have the authority of Jesus to resist the devil. Do it, and he'll turn tail and run!

Have you noticed a pattern in the way the devil attacks or tempts you? If so, what is it?

DAY 92

WHY GOD GAVE PROPHECIES

These things happened so that the scripture would be fulfilled: "Not one of his bones will be broken," and, as another scripture says, "They will look on the one they have pierced."

JOHN 19:36-37

Hundreds of years before Jesus was born, God gave his prophets many prophecies about Jesus—and those things came to pass. For example, you know that Jesus was crucified, right? Now, when the Romans wanted a crucified man to die quickly, they broke his legs. But since Jesus was already dead, they didn't break his bones. Instead, they pierced his side with a spear. Two prophecies fulfilled at once!

So what does this mean to you? Well, it shows that God was thinking of you when he wrote the Bible. He knew you'd have questions like, "What proof is there that God exists? Is

Jesus really who he said he was?" So right when the Bible was being written—centuries before Jesus was even born—God included some prophecies to help convince curious kids like you.

There's more: King David wrote Psalm 22 a thousand years before Jesus' birth—back before people even practiced crucifixion—yet that prophetic psalm perfectly describes what happened to Jesus when he was on the cross, with his arms being pulled out of joint. (See Matthew 27:32–50.) And if you really want your brain boggled, read Isaiah chapter 53. It was written six hundred years before Jesus, yet explains that he would die to forgive our sins.

Fulfilled Bible prophecies are proof that God exists and that Jesus is the Savior of the world. And there are lots of these fulfilled prophecies in the Bible!

What evidence do you see that God keeps his promises?

DAY 93

IN IT FOR THE LONG HAUL

Let us throw off everything that hinders and the sin that so easily entangles. And let us run with perseverance the race marked out for us.

HEBREWS 12:1

This verse compares Christian life to running a race—a long race, that is. In fact, it's such a long race that it'll take your whole life to run it. It's not like a 100-meter sprint to glory. It's more like the Boston Marathon. You wouldn't expect to win that race if you carried a TV on your back, right? So throw off every weight that hinders you.

Paul also said, "I do not run like someone running aimlessly" (1 Corinthians 9:26). It's not like you're going wild, scrambling through a corn maze, and trying to figure out where the path is. In this race the path is marked out for us. The Bible marks the boundary lines clearly—real clearly. But the race is long, so you need to persevere (per-se-veer). That means to keep at something, stick to it, and not give up.

How do you persevere? By keeping your eyes focused on Jesus. Jesus is standing at the finish line, waiting to give you the prize. Also remember that Jesus ran this race already and didn't let anything stop him. Now he's sending his Spirit to help you—so don't give up!

Keep your eyes focused on Jesus—keep your eyes on the prize—and that'll give you the perseverance you need to run the race.

What are some helpful things you can do when you feel tempted to give up?

KEEP YOUR EYES FOCUSED ON JESUS—KEEP YOUR EYES ON THE PRIZE—AND THAT'LL GIVE YOU THE PERSEVERANCE YOU NEED TO RUN THE RACE.

DAY 94

WHEN ADVICE ISN'T APPRECIATED

Do not throw your pearls to pigs. If you do, they may trample them under their feet, and then turn and tear you to pieces.

MATTHEW 7:6

Jesus taught his disciples to speak the truth and proclaim the message boldly, but he also advised them to use wisdom and not to waste their words—which he compared to precious pearls—on unreceptive or ignorant people. Some people simply don't want to hear the gospel, don't want to be told that they should change, and just get mad at those who tell them the truth.

Sometimes you see some kid doing bad stuff and know you should say something—so you do. But what if he threatens to pound you if you don't stop giving him advice? Should you keep on talking, or do you turn off the tap? That's not easy if you're hot under the collar and really want to give the guy a piece of your mind. And you don't always have a message from God, right? Sometimes the kid's just doing something that bugs you.

Don't waste your words on the ignorant. Not only will they resent what you say, but they might actually get physical about it. So if you're giving unwanted advice or telling someone off, pick up on the signals when your advice isn't wanted, know when to stop, and avoid getting your nose punched.

You have to tell people the truth. But you also need to have common sense and stop talking when it's clear that people really, really don't want to listen.

What are some commonsense ways to tell when someone doesn't want to hear your advice?

DAY 95

HELPING JESUS

Truly, I tell you, whatever you did for one of the least of these brothers and sisters of mine, you did for me.

MATTHEW 25:40

When Jesus returns he will reward those who have done good, praising them for feeding him when he was hungry, for giving him clothing when he needed it, for caring for him when he was sick, and for visiting him when he was in jail. People will ask, "When did I do those things for you?" Jesus will reply that whatever we did for anyone who believes in him we did for him.

Now, if you could travel back in time to Israel and you were sitting down eating lunch and you saw Jesus walking by, and he was hungry, would you share your lunch with him? Sure you would! Or if you came by his camp by night when Jesus and his disciples were sleeping under the olive trees, and Jesus was cold, would you loan him your sleeping bag?

Sure, you'd do these things for Jesus. You'd jump at the opportunity. Well, you do have the opportunity. No, Jesus isn't sleeping under the trees anymore, but when you donate your unused clothes to charity or give food to a soup kitchen or visit a sick friend in the hospital, it's the same as doing it for Jesus himself. If Jesus loves some kid enough to send his Holy Spirit to live in his heart, then he surely wants you to be kind to him, even if he's the un-coolest kid you know.

What are some ways you can serve and "help Jesus" today?

DAY 96

REVELATIONS FROM THE BIBLE

Open my eyes that I may see wonderful things in your law.

PSALM 119:18

We don't know who wrote this prayer. King David didn't sign his name to this psalm so it probably wasn't him. But whoever it was, he considered God's Word his greatest treasure. To him, the Scriptures were like a gold mine. He was constantly digging in them. Sure, he'd read them many times, but he prayed for God to open his eyes so he could see wonderful stuff there that he'd never seen before.

Ever been looking for an eraser or a pencil sharpener and you just can't find it? Then your mom walks in the room and points it out to you, like, in five seconds? It was there all along, but you just didn't see it. Well, God's Spirit is like a supermom who can show you stuff in the Bible. God can reveal stuff even to you. You just need to let him open your eyes.

Jesus promised, "The Holy Spirit . . . will teach you all things" (John 14:26). Of course, the Holy Spirit usually uses the Bible to teach you. Let's say you've read John chapter 15 a dozen times already, but then God lifts your eyelids and suddenly it's like you're reading it for the first time. A verse you've read before jumps out at you and suddenly makes sense. Then you say, "Wow! I never saw that before!" You just saw wonderful things in God's Word.

Don't just read your Bible half-asleep because it's something you must do. Ask God to open your eyes and make the read worthwhile.

Next time you read your Bible, pause before you begin and ask God to teach you.

DAY 97

BECOMING MORE LIKE JESUS

When Moses came down from Mount Sinai . . . he was not aware that his face was radiant because he had spoken with the Lord.

EXODUS 34:29

Moses climbed up to the top of Mount Sinai and spent forty days and forty nights there, talking to God. After the Lord gave Moses the Ten Commandments, he sent Moses back down the mountain to the Israelites. Moses showed up and suddenly everyone was backing away, afraid to come near. He didn't realize that his face was glowing with God's glory.

If you spend time praying and reading your Bible, God begins to change you, and you become radiant too. You won't start glowing as bright as Moses did, but you will change. You may be saying, "Hold on! This is talking about holy people like missionaries and people who pray all day—not kids like me!

God doesn't give skateboarders and computer gamers a touch of glory, does he? Does he?"

Oh yeah, he does. You may not think you radiate much of God's presence, but if you're a Christian, his Holy Spirit lives in you. And God's Spirit is constantly changing you, making you more like Jesus all the time. Instead of walking around full of anger or hate or fear, you'll have God's peace and joy in your face. Even if you can't see it, others will. Spend time with God and read your Bible and meditate on it. God's Spirit inside you will become more evident in your life. You will change. Guaranteed.

Can you see ways God has already changed you? If so, how?

SPEND TIME WITH GOD AND READ YOUR BIBLE AND MEDITATE ON IT. GOD'S SPIRIT INSIDE YOU WILL BECOME MORE EVIDENT IN YOUR LIFE.

DAY 98

TEMPORARY TROUBLE, HUGE REWARDS

Our light and momentary troubles are achieving for us an eternal glory that far outweighs them all.

2 CORINTHIANS 4:17

Back in Paul's day, Christians were often persecuted for their faith. People hated them, told lies about them, spat on them, and gave them grief. Sometimes Christians lost their jobs just because of their faith, and they didn't know where they'd get money. Paul knew these troubles were real. After all, he'd suffered a lot himself. But he reminded Christians that these troubles were light because their heavenly rewards would far outweigh the trouble.

It's no fun going through difficult times. Maybe you've lost a good friend or you've been injured. Or maybe your parents are having a hard time financially and you can't afford things that other kids enjoy. Or maybe kids who were once your friends tease you because you believe in Jesus. It may not seem like your troubles are light. They may seem sandbag-heavy.

But God promises that when you suffer here on earth in his name, he will repay you with heavenly rewards, with "an eternal glory that far outweighs them all." Those eternal rewards won't just outweigh your troubles; they'll far outweigh them. It would be like if you missed out on a candy bar now but got a dirt bike in three months. It's worth the wait.

Sometimes when you're going through troubles, it's not easy to keep your eyes on the ultimate goal—heaven. It's not easy to tell yourself that it will be worth it all. But just the same, it will be worth it all.

When you're going through tough times, what are some good ways to encourage yourself?

DAY 99

DUMPING ANGER

Get rid of all bitterness, rage and anger, brawling and slander . . . Be kind and compassionate to one another, forgiving each other just as in Christ God forgave you.

EPHESIANS 4:31-32

God's idea of a "real man" is different than what you see in movies where some guy trash-talks his opponent while slugging the daylights out of him. God's ideal is not an angry guy full of rage (violent anger). Nor does he want you to slander (speak evil of others) or go wild brawling (fighting noisily). He says to get rid of all that.

You might have a quick temper and think you just can't help it: You're gonna blow up no matter what. Sure, it's easy to let your emotions go and rage like a wounded bear, but that usually just gets people angry with you. Hurt them and they'll figure out ways to get back at you and turn others against you as well. It doesn't pan out in the end if you go through life angry.

You can get rid of anger. Decide ahead of time that

you'll control yourself. Pray and ask God to give you love and patience, then bite your tongue. No, you shouldn't just stand by calmly if some little kid is being beat up. There's a time to step in and take action. But there's no sense lashing out in anger if someone simply makes a dumb mistake.

And notice the end of that verse, the most important part of it. We should do this not only because it will make our lives easier, but because it is part of becoming the people Christ calls us to be.

Are there specific things you feel angry about? What's a healthy way to get rid of that anger?

DAY 100

LIVING IN JESUS

So then, just as you received Christ Jesus as Lord, continue to live your lives in him, rooted and built up in him, strengthened in the faith as you were taught.

COLOSSIANS 2:6-7

When you become a Christian, you're doing more than just believing that Jesus died to save you. You're also stating that he's your Lord and Master. Your brother or sister may not be the boss of you, but Jesus definitely is. He's the Son of God, he rules the entire universe, and you're a dot on a little planet called Earth. Just so you have that straight.

Now, this passage is saying that after you receive Jesus and become saved, you need to continue to remember that Jesus is Lord. He didn't change, after all. He's still the Son of God. He's still ruling the universe. And what does it mean to you personally when you realize Jesus is Lord? Well, it means that you will obey him and follow his teachings. How do you do that?

You need to continue to "live in him." Sink your roots deep

down into Jesus. Stay plugged into Jesus and his power. Read the Bible. That way you'll not only be spiritually strong but you'll know what you believe and you'll clue into how he wants you to live.

Live in Jesus. He said in John 15:4, "Remain in me, as I also remain in you." And when you do that, Jesus gives you the power to live the Christian life.

Why is it important to remember that to live the Christian life we need to "remain in Jesus"?